LOVE *with* P.U.L.S.E
PRAISE, UNDERSTAND, LISTEN, SELF REGULATE, EMPATHIZE®

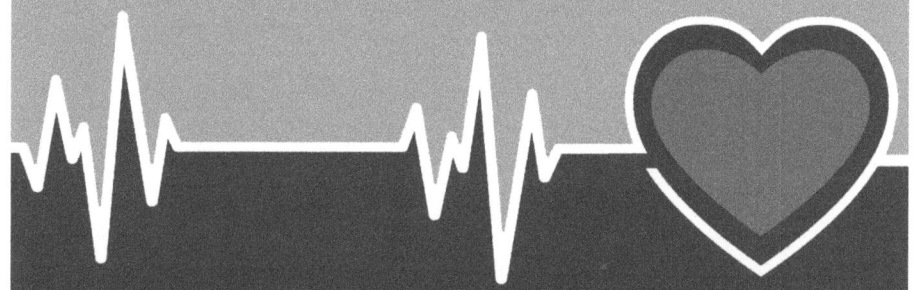

HOW TO CREATE
THE COMMUNICATION AND INTIMACY
YOU CRAVE IN YOUR RELATIONSHIP

ASHLEY R. BRYANT, PHD

Copyright © 2024 by Ashley R. Bryant PhD

All rights reserved.

No portion of this book may be reproduced in any form without written permission from the publisher or author, except as permitted by U.S. copyright law.

This publication is designed to provide accurate and authoritative information in regard to the subject matter covered. It is sold with the understanding that neither the author nor the publisher is engaged in rendering legal, investment, accounting or other professional services. While the publisher and author have used their best efforts in preparing this book, they make no representations or warranties with respect to the accuracy or completeness of the contents of this book and specifically disclaim any implied warranties of merchantability or fitness for a particular purpose. No warranty may be created or extended by sales representatives or written sales materials. The advice and strategies contained herein may not be suitable for your situation. You should consult with a professional when appropriate. Neither the publisher nor the author shall be liable for any loss of profit or any other commercial damages, including but not limited to special, incidental, consequential, personal, or other damages.

Contents

Introduction	1
1. The Heartbeat of Connection	6
2. Praise: The Surprising Superpower in Your Relationship	20
3. Understand: Seeing Through Your Partner's Eyes	39
4. Listen: The Art of Hearing Hearts, Not Just Words	58
5. Self-Regulate: Mastering Your Inner Storms to Create Outer Calm	78
6. Empathize: The Heart of Connection	104
Fullpage image	127
7. Conflict as Connection	128
8. Building Intimacy Beyond Romance	146
9. Building a Shared Vision	169
10. Cultivating Resilience as a Couple	191
11. Celebrating Wins: The Art of Savoring Success Together	213
Fullpage image	232

12. The Role of Self-Growth in Relationships	233
Fullpage image	240
13. Supporting Mental and Emotional Well-Being	241
Fullpage image	263
14. Managing Stress Together	264
Fullpage image	288
15. The P.U.L.S.E. Journey Continues	289
Fullpage image	311
Afterword	312

Introduction

How to Embark on Your P.U.L.S.E. Journey

Welcome to Love with P.U.L.S.E.! You're holding more than just a book; this is an invitation to a transformative journey, a practical guide designed to help you and your partner cultivate a deeper, more resilient, and profoundly intimate connection. Whether your relationship is facing turbulent waters, or you simply yearn to strengthen an already good bond, the P.U.L.S.E. framework within these pages offers potent insights and actionable tools for lasting growth and rediscovery.

To truly unlock the potential of Love with P.U.L.S.E., I encourage you to approach it not as a passive read, but as an active, heartfelt exploration. This book is structured to guide you, step by step, through the core principles that can revitalize your relationship. You'll discover the P.U.L.S.E. framework, a unique approach focusing on Praise, Understanding, Listening, Self-regulation, and Empathy, and learn how these elements, when woven into the fabric of your daily interactions, can create extraordinary shifts.

Inside, you will find:

- **Core Concepts:** Each principle of the P.U.L.S.E.

framework is explored in depth, helping you understand the 'why' behind the 'how.' You'll learn not just what to do, but why these practices matter and how they work to strengthen your connection.

- **Practical Exercises:** This is where the magic happens. You'll be invited to engage with thoughtfully designed exercises, tailored to help you and your partner practice and internalize these new skills. These range from simple daily actions to more profound explorations, allowing you to progress at your own pace. Each chapter concludes with reflection questions and specific activities designed to reinforce the concepts in real world application.

- **Real-Life Insights:** Drawing from years of experience and relatable stories, this book aims to make the path to a stronger relationship clear and achievable. You'll find case studies of couples who have successfully navigated challenges using these principles, offering both inspiration and practical examples of the framework in action.

- **Dialogue Scripts:** Throughout the book, you'll find sample conversations that demonstrate how to apply the P.U.L.S.E. principles in everyday interactions. These scripts serve as models that you can adapt to your own unique relationship dynamics.

Think of this book as your companion and coach. Engage with the material, underline passages that resonate, discuss the concepts with your partner, and most importantly, commit to trying the exercises. The journey to a more connected love is built on small, consistent efforts. There's no magic wand, but there is the power of intentional practice.

As you move through these pages, remember that every relationship is unique, and so is its path to growth. Be patient with yourselves, celebrate the small victories, and embrace the process of learning and evolving together. The P.U.L.S.E. framework is designed to be flexible, allowing you to adapt its wisdom to your specific circumstances and challenges.

How to Use This Book

For maximum benefit, I recommend the following approach:

1. Read Together if Possible: While you can certainly benefit from this book on your own, the impact is multiplied when both partners engage with the material. Consider setting aside time to read and discuss each chapter together.

2. Take Your Time: Don't rush through the content. Each chapter builds upon the previous one, and the exercises are designed to be practiced over time. Allow yourselves the space to integrate these new skills before moving on.

3. Be Honest with Yourselves: The exercises in this book invite vulnerability and honesty. Create a safe space for open communication, free from judgment or criticism.

4. Commit to Practice: Like any skill worth having, the principles in the P.U.L.S.E. framework require practice. Commit to implementing what you learn, even when it feels challenging.

5. Return to Chapters as Needed: As your relationship evolves, you may find that different aspects of the framework become more relevant. Feel free to revisit chapters that speak to your current challenges or goals.

Are you ready to feel the pulse of your relationship quicken with new understanding and affection? Let's begin this journey together. You have the capacity to build the love you desire, and this book is here to show you how.

The P.U.L.S.E. Framework at a Glance

Before we dive into each component in detail, here's a brief overview of what P.U.L.S.E. stands for:

P - Praise: Learning to genuinely acknowledge and appreciate your partner, creating a culture of gratitude and recognition in your relationship.

U - Understand: Developing the ability to see situations from your partner's perspective, even when it differs from your own.

L - Listen: Mastering the art of active, empathetic listening that goes beyond hearing words to understanding feelings and needs.

S - Self-regulate: Building skills to manage your own emotional responses, especially during conflict or stress.

E - Empathize: Cultivating deep emotional connection through shared feelings and experiences.

Each of these elements works in harmony with the others, creating a comprehensive approach to relationship health and growth. As you progress through this book, you'll discover how these principles interconnect and reinforce each other, creating a powerful foundation for lasting love.

Now, let's begin our exploration with Chapter 1, where we'll examine the fundamental nature of connection and why it matters so deeply in our relationships.

Chapter 1
The Heartbeat of Connection

Love. It's a word that echoes through the deepest chambers of our hearts, a fundamental human need that shapes our lives, fuels our dreams, and, at times, brings us to our knees. We seek it, celebrate it, and sometimes, we struggle profoundly with it.

In a world that often feels disconnected, the quest for genuine, lasting connection with a partner is more vital than ever. But let's be honest: navigating the complexities of a longterm relationship can feel like trying to read a map in the dark, especially when the fairytales and filtered social media feeds paint a picture of love that's effortlessly perfect.

If you've ever found yourself wondering why your relationship feels harder than it "should," or if the vibrant spark you once shared seems to have dimmed under the weight of daily life, you are not alone. So many of us embark on the journey of love with hearts full of hope, only to find that the reality of building a life together involves challenges we were never taught how to navigate. We talk endlessly about falling in love, but who teaches us how to stay in love, how to nurture it, and how to help it grow stronger through the inevitable storms?

The Alluring Myth of Effortless Love

Remember those early days? The intoxicating rush of new love, where every touch sent shivers down your spine, conversations flowed effortlessly into the early hours of the morning, and you felt like you'd finally found your other half. It's a beautiful, exhilarating phase, often fueled by a potent cocktail of brain chemistry – dopamine, oxytocin, serotonin – that makes the world seem brighter and your connection feel unbreakable. You finish each other's sentences, share the same quirky sense of humor, and believe you can conquer anything as long as you're together.

This is the magic that popular culture idolizes, the "happily ever after" that often ends the story right when the real work—and the real beauty—begins. The unspoken belief is that if it's "meant to be," it will be easy. This is the myth of effortless love, a seductive idea that can unfortunately set us up for disappointment and self-doubt when the initial intensity naturally begins to settle.

Life, in all its messy glory, intervenes. Careers demand our energy, financial pressures mount, family responsibilities grow, and the simple rhythm of day-to-day routines can begin to overshadow those initial highs. The very habits and ways of being that once felt so natural can start to feel like effort. It's at this point that many couples begin to wonder if something is fundamentally wrong, if the spark has died, or if they've somehow failed at love.

Case Study: The Reality Check

Sarah and Michael had been married for three years when they first came to my office. Their story was one I'd heard many times before: a whirlwind romance, a beautiful wedding, and then the gradual realization that marriage wasn't the fairytale they'd expected.

"We used to talk for hours," Sarah explained, her voice tinged with nostalgia. "Now it feels like we're just roommates passing each other in the hallway."

Michael nodded in agreement. "I love her, but sometimes I wonder if we made a mistake. It shouldn't be this hard, should it?"

This question—"It shouldn't be this hard, should it?"—is perhaps one of the most common I hear in my practice. It reveals the powerful grip that the myth of effortless love has on our collective psyche.

Over several sessions, Sarah and Michael began to understand that their struggles weren't a sign of failure, but rather an invitation to grow together. They learned that the transition from passionate romance to a deeper, more sustainable love requires new skills and understanding—precisely what the P.U.L.S.E. framework offers.

I remember this vividly from my own marriage. When I first said "I do" in my early twenties, my husband and I were young, deeply in love, and admittedly, rather clueless about what it truly meant to build a life together. We'd reconnected a few years after a youthful ghosting episode on his part (yes, it happens to the best of us!), and after a whirlwind three months of dating, there we were, exchanging vows. We loved each other immensely, but we stepped into marriage armed with a lot of passion and very few practical communication skills. The early years, while filled with love, were also punctuated by frequent arguments and misunderstandings. We were navigating by instinct, often bumping into the same relational roadblocks, wondering why something that felt so right could also be so challenging.

What I've learned since, both as a therapist guiding countless couples and through the ongoing journey of my own marriage, is that this shift from effortless romance to a more complex reality isn't a sign of failure. Instead, it's an invitation. It's the point where the initial chemistry makes way for something far deeper and more resilient: a conscious, intentional connection built on understanding, effort, and a shared commitment to growth. And that, my friend, is where the true adventure of lasting love begins. It's where the P.U.L.S.E. framework can become your compass.

Introducing the P.U.L.S.E. Framework: Your Compass for Connection

My own early marital struggles, and the countless stories I've heard from couples in my therapy practice, highlighted a universal truth: love alone, without the right tools and understanding, often isn't enough to sustain a thriving partnership through the complexities of life. We needed more than just good intentions; we needed a practical approach, a kind of roadmap to navigate the inevitable challenges and to consciously cultivate the connection we craved. This realization was the seed from which the P.U.L.S.E. Framework grew.

It became clear that so much of the disconnection and pain in relationships stemmed from common patterns: feeling unheard, misunderstood, unappreciated, or overwhelmed by conflict.

Communication wasn't just about talking; it was about the quality of that talking, the listening, the empathy, and the ability to manage our own emotional storms so we could show up for our partners in a constructive way. You've heard it said that "communication is key," right? It's almost a cliché. But let's expand that: effective communication, in its richest sense, isn't just a key. It's the master key that unlocks deeper intimacy, trust, and resilience. It encompasses not just the words we say, but our ability to truly listen, to understand our partner's world, to express appreciation genuinely, to manage our own reactions during tense moments, and to connect with empathy.

The P.U.L.S.E. Framework, which stands for Praise, Understand, Listen, Self-regulate, and Empathize was born from this understanding. It's not a rigid set of rules, but a set of guiding principles, a compass designed to help you and your partner navigate back to each other, again and again. It's built on years of psychological research, insights from successful couples, and the very real, often messy, experiences of learning to love better.

The Science Behind P.U.L.S.E.

The P.U.L.S.E. framework isn't just intuitive—it's backed by decades of relationship research. Studies by relationship experts like Dr. John Gottman have consistently shown that successful couples share certain communication patterns and emotional skills:

1. They maintain a positive perspective: Research shows that thriving relationships have a ratio of at least 5 positive interactions to every negative one. This is where Praise becomes essential.

2. They seek to understand before being understood: Couples who make an effort to see things from their partner's perspective report higher relationship satisfaction. This is the Understand component.

3. They practice active listening: Studies demonstrate that feeling truly heard is one of the strongest predictors of relationship success. Hence the Listen element.

4. They manage their emotional responses: Research on emotional regulation shows that partners who

can calm themselves during conflict have more productive conversations and faster reconciliation. This is Self-regulation in action.

5. They connect emotionally: The ability to share in your partner's emotional experience—Empathize—creates a profound bond that strengthens resilience against life's challenges.

This framework is designed to address the core needs within a relationship: the need to feel seen, heard, valued, and safe. It provides a shared language and a set of actionable skills that can transform how you interact, especially when life gets tough. It's about moving from reactive patterns, where we might unintentionally hurt each other, to intentional connection, where we consciously choose behaviors that strengthen our bond.

Why This Journey of Effort is Profoundly Worth It

Let's be clear: embarking on the P.U.L.S.E. journey, or any conscious effort to improve your relationship, requires exactly that – effort. In a world that often sells us quick fixes and instant gratification, the idea of "working" on our love lives can sometimes feel daunting. Why bother when society whispers that true love should just be?

Here's why: the rewards of investing in your relationship are among the most profound and life-enhancing you can experience. A strong, healthy partnership isn't just a source of comfort and joy; it's a bedrock for your overall well-being. It impacts your physical health, your mental and emotional resilience, your sense of purpose, and even your longevity.

When you commit to understanding and applying principles like those in the P.U.L.S.E. framework, you're not just learning to "fix" problems; you're building something extraordinary. You are cultivating:

Deeper Intimacy: Beyond the physical, you're fostering emotional and intellectual closeness, a sense of being truly known and accepted by your partner.

Unshakeable Trust: Consistent effort in understanding, listening, and empathizing builds a foundation of safety and reliability that allows both partners to be vulnerable and authentic.

Enhanced Resilience: Life will inevitably throw curveballs. A relationship strengthened by shared skills and mutual understanding can weather storms that might break a more fragile connection. You become a team that can face adversity together.

Greater Joy and Fulfillment: When you feel truly connected to your partner, the everyday moments become richer, and shared experiences create a tapestry of joyful memories.

A Positive Ripple Effect: The health of your primary relationship often positively impacts other areas of your life, including your relationships with children, friends, and family, and even your professional life.

Real-Life Transformation

David and Elena had been together for twelve years when they decided to try the P.U.L.S.E. approach. Their relationship wasn't in crisis. They weren't considering separation or experiencing major conflict, but they both felt something was missing.

"We love each other," Elena explained, "but sometimes it feels like we're just going through the motions. The spark is gone."

Over the course of several months, they committed to practicing each element of the P.U.L.S.E. framework. They started with small daily expressions of appreciation (Praise), then gradually incorporated the other elements.

Six months later, they reported a profound shift in their relationship. "It's like we've rediscovered each other," David shared. "I feel seen in a way I haven't in years."

Elena agreed: "The most surprising thing is how these small changes have created such a big difference. We're more playful, more intimate, and I feel like we're truly partners again."

Their story illustrates an important truth: even relationships that aren't "broken" can benefit enormously from intentional connection practices.

Think of it like tending a garden. A beautiful, thriving garden doesn't just happen. It requires consistent watering, weeding, nurturing, and attention. The effort involved isn't a sign that the garden is flawed; it's a testament to its value and your commitment to its beauty and abundance. Your relationship is that garden. The P.U.L.S.E. framework offers you the tools and knowledge to tend it with skill and love, so it can flourish and provide a lifetime of nourishment.

This isn't about achieving a "perfect" relationship, because perfection is an illusion. Life is beautifully imperfect, and so are we. The goal isn't to eliminate all conflict or disagreement, That's unrealistic and, frankly, a bit boring! Instead, the goal is to learn how to navigate those challenges with grace, to repair effectively, to keep your connection alive and vibrant even when things are tough, and to continuously choose each other. It's about building a love that is not just passionate, but also peaceful, playful, and profoundly present.

Chapter Reflection: Examining Your Relationship Pulse

Take a moment to reflect on your own relationship journey. Where do you feel the strongest connection with your partner? Where do you sense disconnection? Consider these questions individually, then share your thoughts with each other if you're working through this book together:

1. What initially drew you to your partner? What

qualities did you most admire?

2. When do you feel most connected to your partner now? Describe specific moments or activities.

3. What areas of your relationship would you like to strengthen?

4. On a scale of 1-10, how would you rate the current level of effort you put into nurturing your relationship? How about your partner?

5. What's one small step you could take today to strengthen your connection?

Practice Exercise: Connection Inventory

Time needed: 20-30 minutes **Materials:** Notebook or journal, pen
Individually, create a "connection inventory" by listing: - Three moments in the past month when you felt deeply connected to your partner - Three situations where you felt disconnected or misunderstood - Three specific actions that help you feel more connected (these can be things you do or things your partner does)
If you're both participating, share your lists with each other without judgment or defensiveness. Look for patterns and insights. Are there particular activities or communication styles that consistently strengthen your connection? Are there recurring situations that lead to disconnection?
Use this inventory as a starting point for understanding your unique relationship dynamics and as a reference point as you progress through the P.U.L.S.E. framework.

In the chapters that follow, we will dive into each element of the P.U.L.S.E. framework. You'll find practical exercises, reflection prompts, and real-life examples to help you integrate these principles into your unique relationship. This journey won't always be easy, but it will be transformative. You are investing in the heart of your life, and that is an effort that always repays itself, a thousandfold.

Take a deep breath. Open your heart. Let's begin.

LOVE WITH P.U.L.S.E.

KEEP GOING AFTER THE CHAPTER ENDS

- Guided Video Exercises
- Printable Worksheets
- Real-Life Tools You Can Use Today

Turn what you just read into what you can actually do — right now.

Dr. Ashley R. Bryant

Creator of the P.U.L.S.E. Framework & Author of Love With P.U.L.S.E.

Already finished the book? Scan to access every chapter's bonus content in one place.

Chapter 2
Praise: The Surprising Superpower in Your Relationship

The Secret Sauce of Thriving Relationships

Picture this: it was a few years into my marriage, and if I'm being completely honest, the initial, blazing inferno of newlywed passion had simmered down to a somewhat flickering flame. Don't get me wrong, the love was still there, a deep and abiding current beneath the surface. But the relentless daily grind – work deadlines, bills piling up, the endless cycle of chores (who knew fighting about doing the laundry could become a recurring life theme?) – had undeniably taken its toll. Money was tighter than we liked, spontaneous date nights had become a distant memory, and our conversations, more often than not, revolved around the mundane logistics of life or, let's face it, complaining about our jobs.

It was during one of those "is this all there is?" phases that I stumbled across the movie "Fireproof." For those who haven't seen it, it's a story about a husband who, facing a crumbling marriage, embarks on a 40-day journey of intentional acts of love and kindness, guided by advice from a wise older mentor. Now, I'm generally not one for overly sentimental movies, but as cheesy as it might sound, something about that story resonated deeply with me. I found myself unexpectedly tearing up at the end, watching the husband's consistent, heartfelt efforts slowly melt his wife's understandably icy heart.

That movie was a wake-up call. It hit me with the force of a revelation: if we weren't careful, my husband and I could easily slip into that dangerous, soul-eroding cycle of taking each other for granted, of letting the small irritations overshadow the deep love that brought us together. So, right then and there, tissues still clutched in my hand, I made a decision. Instead of cataloging all the things that weren't perfect, instead of focusing on the ways our relationship felt strained or what I wished was different – a habit that, if I'm honest, had started to creep in – I was going to become fiercely intentional about expressing gratitude. Every single day.

I vowed to start actively looking for and acknowledging the good. I'd thank my husband for the small, everyday acts of service – like that one miraculous time he cleaned the entire house without a single prompt (yes, miracles do happen, folks!). And I promised myself I'd make a point to vocalize my appreciation for the bigger sacrifices, like his unwavering willingness to work long, grueling hours at a job that, at the time, was draining his spirit, all to provide for our family.

Looking back, I'm sure my initial attempts at this newfound "praise offensive" were probably a bit awkward, maybe even a little forced. It likely felt like a teenager fumbling through their first attempt at flirting. "Oh, um, thanks for... doing the dishes last night. That was... sweet of you." Smooth, I know. But to my husband's immense credit, he never once made fun of my slightly clumsy efforts or brushed off my expressions of gratitude. If anything, I began to see a subtle shift, a little sparkle returning to his eyes with each "thank you." It was like watching a wilted flower finally receive the water it so desperately needed.

The Transformative Power of Appreciation

As the days turned into weeks, something truly amazing began to unfold. Those once stilted words of praise started to flow more naturally, more spontaneously, from a place of genuine appreciation and rekindled tenderness. Suddenly, I wasn't just looking for things to praise; I was seeing them everywhere. I found myself spontaneously thanking him for the way he always knew how to make me laugh, even when I was stressed to the gills, my heart swelling with a familiar warmth and affection. Or I'd find myself sincerely complimenting the quiet kindness he showed a flustered server during a rare dinner out, feeling a surge of pride and deep admiration for the incredible, good-hearted man I had chosen to share my life with.

For this personal goal of mine, this quest to cultivate a culture of appreciation, I didn't set a 40-day limit like in the movie. I simply made it my mission to find something to praise, something to be grateful for, every single day. And you know what happened? It became contagious. My husband started doing the same for me. We fell into this beautiful, life-affirming rhythm of lifting each other up, of celebrating the small wins and the quiet acts of love that are the true bedrock of a partnership. Now, over fifteen years later, that culture of praise and gratitude is still a vibrant, essential part of our marriage. Sure, we still have our fair share of squabbles, disagreements, and the occasional exasperated eye-roll (because let's be real, what long-term couple doesn't?). But at the end of the day, we always find our way back to appreciation. A simple, heartfelt "thank you for being such an amazing husband" or "I really appreciate how hard you work for us" can be like a relationship defibrillator, shocking our love back to its full, vibrant life, especially when the stresses of life try to make it flat-line.

I share this deeply personal story not to present a picture of a perfect marriage, but to illustrate the profound, almost magical power of praise. What began as a somewhat contrived, movie-inspired attempt to safeguard my marriage ended up becoming one of the most vital ingredients in making it truly thrive. And here's the crucial thing: my experience isn't just a fluke, a one-off anecdote. The transformative power of praise is backed by a fascinating body of scientific research.

The Science of Praise: Why It Works So Powerfully

Psychologically and neurologically, praise isn't just a "nice-to-have" in a relationship; it's a fundamental nutrient for connection and well-being. Our brains are literally wired to respond to positive reinforcement. When we give or receive genuine praise, a complex and wonderful cascade of neurochemical processes is set in motion.

When you express sincere appreciation to your partner, both of your brains experience a surge of dopamine, often dubbed the "feel-good" neurotransmitter. Dopamine is associated with pleasure, reward, and motivation. This release of dopamine reinforces the positive feeling connected to the praised behavior or quality, making both you and your partner more likely to want to repeat those positive actions and interactions. It's a beautiful, self-reinforcing cycle: praise feels good, so we do more of what elicits praise, which leads to more praise, and so on.

Beyond the immediate pleasure hit, dopamine plays a crucial role in motivation and learning. The more consistently we are praised for something positive, the more intrinsically motivated we become to continue that behavior. In the context of a relationship, this can create a powerful virtuous cycle. By consistently acknowledging and appreciating your partner's positive qualities and actions, you're essentially training both of your brains to focus more on the positive aspects of your relationship.

Research Spotlight: The Gottman Institute

Dr. John Gottman, one of the world's leading researchers on marital stability and relationship success, has found that in thriving relationships, couples maintain a "magic ratio" of at least five positive interactions to every negative one. These positive interactions include expressions of appreciation, affection, and respect—all forms of praise.

Gottman's research, conducted over decades with thousands of couples, revealed that this 5:1 ratio is one of the most reliable predictors of relationship satisfaction and longevity. Couples who consistently fall below this ratio are significantly more likely to experience relationship distress and, ultimately, separation.

What's particularly fascinating is that this ratio holds true across different cultures, ages, and relationship lengths. It appears to be a fundamental principle of human connection, not just a cultural or generational preference.

The Neuroscience of Appreciation

Recent advances in neuroscience have given us remarkable insights into why praise and appreciation are so powerful in relationships. When we receive genuine appreciation from our partner, several important brain regions activate:

1. **The Ventral Striatum**: This reward center of the brain lights up in response to praise, releasing dopamine

that creates feelings of pleasure and reinforces the connection between the relationship and positive emotions.

2. **The Medial Prefrontal Cortex**: This region, involved in our sense of self, activates when we receive authentic praise, strengthening our positive self-concept within the relationship.

3. **The Anterior Cingulate Cortex**: This area helps regulate emotional responses and shows increased activity during positive social interactions like receiving appreciation.

Research using functional MRI has shown that these brain regions don't just activate momentarily. Regular experiences of appreciation can actually strengthen neural pathways, creating what neuroscientists call "experience-dependent neuroplasticity." In simpler terms, consistent praise literally reshapes your brain's physical structure to become more attuned to positive aspects of your relationship.

Dr. Barbara Fredrickson's research on positive emotions provides another fascinating perspective. Her "broaden-and-build" theory suggests that positive emotions like those generated through praise and appreciation expand our awareness and build enduring personal resources. In relationships, this means that regular appreciation helps partners notice more positive aspects of each other and builds resilience against future challenges.

The Gender Factor: Do Men and Women Respond Differently to Praise?

A question that often arises in my therapy sessions is whether men and women have different needs when it comes to praise. While individual differences always outweigh gender generalizations, research does suggest some interesting patterns worth considering.

Studies indicate that men often place high value on praise related to their competence, provision abilities, and achievements. This doesn't mean that men don't appreciate emotional affirmation. They absolutely do, but recognition of their efforts, skills, and contributions tends to resonate deeply.

Women, on the other hand, often report valuing praise that acknowledges both their competence and their emotional contributions to the relationship. Appreciation for nurturing behaviors, emotional support, and relationship maintenance efforts can be particularly meaningful.

However, it's crucial to note that these are broad patterns, not rigid rules. The most effective approach is to learn your specific partner's "praise language"—what forms of appreciation resonate most deeply with them as an individual.

Case Study: Michael and Jennifer

Michael and Jennifer had been married for eight years when they came to therapy. Their primary complaint was feeling disconnected and under appreciated by each other.

During our sessions, we discovered that Michael had been working extra hours to save for a family vacation—something he thought would make Jennifer happy. He felt hurt that she didn't seem to notice or appreciate his sacrifice. Jennifer, meanwhile, had been making extra efforts to keep their home running smoothly and to be emotionally available to Michael despite her own work stress. She felt her efforts were invisible to him.

The problem wasn't that they didn't appreciate each other. It was that they weren't expressing that appreciation in ways that resonated with their partner. Michael needed verbal acknowledgment of his provision efforts, while Jennifer needed recognition of her emotional labor and household management.

We worked on tailoring their expressions of gratitude to match their partner's needs. Within weeks, both reported feeling significantly more valued and connected. Jennifer started specifically thanking Michael for his hard work and provision, while Michael began noticing and appreciating Jennifer's emotional support and home management efforts.

Their story illustrates an important point: effective praise isn't one-size-fits-all. It requires understanding what matters most to your specific partner.

Attachment Theory and the Power of Praise

Attachment theory, pioneered by John Bowlby and Mary Ainsworth, provides another lens for understanding why praise is so powerful in relationships. According to attachment theory, we all have fundamental needs for security, validation, and reassurance in our close relationships.

Dr. Sue Johnson, founder of Emotionally Focused Therapy, explains that positive affirmation helps create what she calls a "secure attachment bond" between partners. When we consistently praise and appreciate our partners, we're essentially sending the message: "I see you. You matter to me. You are valued and important." These messages directly address our deepest attachment needs.

For individuals with anxious attachment tendencies (those who worry about abandonment or rejection), regular praise can be particularly healing, as it provides reassurance about their value in the relationship. For those with avoidant attachment patterns (those who tend to maintain emotional distance), praise that respects their competence while gently acknowledging emotional connection can help build trust and security.

Research by Dr. Jeffry Simpson has shown that secure attachment in adult relationships is associated with higher levels of expressed appreciation between partners. This creates a virtuous cycle: secure attachment facilitates more praise, and more praise strengthens secure attachment.

The Five Languages of Praise: Finding Your Partner's Dialect

Just as we each have a primary "love language" (as popularized by Dr. Gary Chapman), we also tend to have preferred ways of receiving praise. Understanding your partner's praise preferences can dramatically increase the impact of your appreciation efforts. Here are five common "praise languages" I've observed in my practice:

1. **Verbal Affirmation**: Some people primarily value direct, spoken words of appreciation. "I'm so grateful for how you always make time to listen to me" or "I really admire how hard you work for our family" can be deeply meaningful to these individuals.

2. **Recognition of Effort**: For others, acknowledgment of their hard work and sacrifice resonates most strongly. "I noticed how much effort you put into planning that dinner" or "I appreciate how you took on that difficult conversation with the kids so I didn't have to" speaks volumes.

3. **Public Acknowledgment**: Some individuals feel especially valued when their partner praises them in front of others. A simple "Have I told you all what an amazing cook my husband is?" at a dinner party can

fill their emotional tank.

4. **Written Appreciation**: For certain people, written words carry special weight. A thoughtful text message, a post-it note on the mirror, or a heartfelt card can be treasured expressions of appreciation.

5. **Specific Over General**: While some are content with general praise ("You're wonderful"), others need specific recognition ("I love how you always remember to ask about my difficult meetings").

The key is to observe which forms of praise seem to light up your partner. When do they seem most touched or responsive? What kinds of appreciation do they tend to give others (as we often give what we hope to receive)? You can even directly ask: "When I appreciate you, what kinds of recognition feel most meaningful to you?"

Common Praise Pitfalls and How to Avoid Them

While praise is powerful, not all expressions of appreciation are created equal. Here are some common pitfalls to avoid:

1. **The Backhanded Compliment**: "You actually did a good job with dinner tonight" or "The house looks nice for once" contains implicit criticism that undermines the praise. Avoid qualifiers like "actually," "for once," or "finally" that suggest surprise at competence.

2. **The Comparison Trap**: "You're so much better at this than Sarah's husband" might seem like high praise, but comparisons often create discomfort rather than appreciation.

3. **The Conditional Compliment**: "I love how you look when you make an effort" suggests your appreciation is conditional on certain behaviors rather than being about the person themselves.

4. **The Exaggeration**: Over-the-top praise that doesn't feel authentic ("You're literally the best cook in the entire world!") can come across as insincere or manipulative.

5. **The Praise Drought**: Perhaps the biggest pitfall is simply forgetting to praise at all, especially during busy or stressful periods when appreciation is most needed.

The antidote to these pitfalls is simple but powerful: be specific, be sincere, be consistent, and be generous. Genuine appreciation, expressed regularly and thoughtfully, is one of the most powerful gifts you can give your relationship.

Exercise: The Daily Appreciation Practice

Time needed: 2-3 minutes daily **Materials:** None
For one week, commit to expressing at least one specific, genuine appreciation to your partner every day. Set a reminder on your phone if needed. At the end of the week, reflect on any changes you've noticed in your relationship dynamic or your own perspective.

_____
_____
_____
_____
_____
_____
_____
_____
_____
_____
_____
_____

Exercise: The Praise Language Discovery

Time needed: 30 minutes Materials: Paper and pen for notes

Have a conversation with your partner specifically about how each of you prefers to receive appreciation. Ask questions like:

- "When was the last time you felt truly appreciated by me? What did I do or say?"

- "What kind of recognition means the most to you—words, gestures, public acknowledgment, or something else?"

- "Is there a form of appreciation you've been missing from me?"

Take notes and commit to incorporating what you learn into your daily interactions.

Dialogue Scripts: Praise in Action

Here are some examples of effective praise in different relationship contexts:

- **For everyday contributions:** "I noticed how you took care of the dishes without being asked tonight. That kind of thoughtfulness really means a lot to me, and it makes our home feel like a true partnership. Thank you for being so considerate."

- **For character qualities:** "You know what I've been thinking about lately? How patient you are with your mom, even when she's being difficult. That kind of compassion is something I really admire about you. It shows what a deeply good person you are."

- **For support during challenges:** "I just want to say how much I appreciate how you supported me through that work crisis last week. You listened when I needed to vent, gave me space when I needed to think, and never made me feel like I was burdening you. Having you in my corner makes all the difference."

- **For physical affirmation:** "I love how you always reach for my hand when we're walking together. That small gesture of connection makes me feel so loved and reminds me that we're a team, even in the simplest moments."

- **For growth and change:** "I've noticed how much effort you've been putting into being more patient with the kids, especially during their bedtime routine. I know that doesn't come naturally, and seeing you work on it shows me how committed you are to being the best parent you can be. It really inspires me."

Chapter Reflection:

Your Praise Journey Take a moment to reflect on praise in your relationship:

1. How often do you express genuine appreciation to your partner? Is praise a regular part of your relationship culture, or has it become rare?

2. What patterns of praise did you observe in your family of origin? How might these influence your current comfort level with giving and receiving appreciation?

3. What aspects of your partner do you appreciate but rarely express? What holds you back from verbalizing these positive feelings more often?

4. How might increasing the frequency and specificity of praise change the emotional climate of your relationship?

5. Which praise practice from this chapter seems most relevant to enhancing your specific relationship right now?

The Bridge to the Next Chapter: From Praise to Understanding

While praise creates a foundation of positive regard and appreciation, truly thriving relationships also require deep understanding. In the next chapter, we'll explore how seeing the world through your partner's eyes—understanding their unique perspective, history, and inner landscape—creates the kind of profound connection that sustains love through life's inevitable challenges.

We'll discover how developing empathetic understanding helps partners navigate differences without judgment, respond to each other's needs with greater accuracy, and create the kind of emotional safety that allows vulnerability to flourish. You'll learn practical approaches to what relationship researchers call "perspective-taking"—the ability to temporarily step out of your own viewpoint to truly grasp your partner's experience.

But before we move on, I encourage you to begin implementing at least one praise practice from this chapter. Remember that neural pathways strengthen through consistent activation—each expression of appreciation literally reshapes your brain's relationship patterns, gradually creating a culture where positivity and gratitude become your default setting rather than something you have to consciously remember to do.

LOVE WITH P.U.L.S.E.

KEEP GOING AFTER THE CHAPTER ENDS

- Guided Video Exercises
- Printable Worksheets
- Real-Life Tools You Can Use Today

Turn what you just read into what you can actually do — right now.

Dr. Ashley R. Bryant

Creator of the P.U.L.S.E. Framework & Author of Love With P.U.L.S.E.

Already finished the book? Scan to access every chapter's bonus content in one place.

Chapter 3
Understand: Seeing Through Your Partner's Eyes

Understanding your partner—truly seeing the world through their eyes—is perhaps one of the most profound gifts you can offer in a relationship. It's also one of the most challenging. When we fall in love, we're often drawn to someone precisely because they're different from us—they bring new perspectives, different strengths, and complementary qualities to our lives. Yet these very differences that initially attract us can become sources of frustration and disconnection when we fail to bridge the gap between our worldviews.

In this chapter, we'll explore the transformative power of understanding in relationships. We'll delve into why it matters so deeply, what prevents us from truly understanding our partners, and most importantly, how to develop this crucial skill as part of the P.U.L.S.E. framework.

The Understanding Gap: Why We Struggle to See Through Our Partner's Eyes

Have you ever found yourself utterly baffled by your partner's reaction to something? Perhaps they became upset over what seemed to you like a minor issue, or they remained calm during what you perceived as a crisis. Maybe they interpreted a comment or situation completely differently than you did, leaving you wondering if you were even experiencing the same reality.

These moments of disconnect aren't unusual—they're actually a normal part of intimate relationships. But understanding why they happen can help us navigate them more effectively.

The Illusion of Objectivity

One of the most fundamental barriers to understanding our partners is what psychologists call "naive realism"—the belief that we see the world objectively, as it truly is, while others who disagree with us must be misinformed, irrational, or biased.

The truth is far more complex: each of us experiences reality through the filter of our unique life experiences, personality traits, cultural background, family dynamics, and countless other factors. There is no single "correct" way to perceive or interpret the world. Your reality and your partner's reality can be dramatically different, and both can be valid simultaneously.

Case Study: The Birthday Dinner Disconnect

Maria and James had been together for three years when they experienced a significant misunderstanding around Maria's birthday. James had planned what he thought was the perfect surprise—a reservation at an exclusive new restaurant downtown, followed by tickets to a jazz show. He was excited to treat Maria to this special evening and had been planning it for weeks.

When the evening arrived, however, Maria seemed increasingly withdrawn and upset. By dessert, she was barely speaking, and James was completely confused. Later that night, when he finally asked what was wrong, Maria explained that she had been hoping for a quiet, intimate dinner at home. She'd had an exhausting week at work and was feeling socially drained. The last thing she wanted was to be in a crowded, noisy restaurant and then attend a show.

James was devastated. "But I thought you'd love it! You always talk about wanting to try new restaurants, and you love jazz!"

"I do," Maria acknowledged, "but not when I'm this exhausted. I just wanted to be alone with you, somewhere quiet where we could really talk."

This scenario illustrates a classic understanding gap. James wasn't wrong about Maria's general preferences, but he missed important contextual factors—her current emotional state and needs. He projected his own interpretation of what would make a perfect birthday (excitement, novelty, special experiences) onto Maria, without considering that her needs might be different, especially given her current circumstances.

The Science of Understanding: Perspective-Taking and Empathic Accuracy

Research in relationship psychology has identified two key components of understanding: perspective-taking (the cognitive ability to see situations from another's viewpoint) and empathic accuracy (the ability to correctly identify what another person is thinking and feeling).

Studies show that couples with higher levels of these skills report greater relationship satisfaction, less conflict, and more effective problem-solving. Interestingly, research also suggests that we tend to overestimate our ability to understand our partners—we think we know them better than we actually do.

This overconfidence can be problematic because it prevents us from asking clarifying questions or seeking to understand when we're confused by our partner's behavior. Instead, we make assumptions based on our own perspective, which often leads to misunderstandings and conflict.

The Neuroscience of Understanding

Recent advances in neuroscience have given us remarkable insights into the biological basis of understanding others. When we attempt to understand our partner's perspective, several important brain regions activate:

   1. **The Temporoparietal Junction (TPJ)**: This region

plays a crucial role in what scientists call "theory of mind" – our ability to attribute mental states, beliefs, and intentions to others. Research using functional MRI has shown that the TPJ activates when we're trying to understand another person's perspective that differs from our own.

2. **The Medial Prefrontal Cortex (mPFC)**: This area is involved in understanding others' mental states and is particularly active when we're thinking about the thoughts and feelings of people we're close to, like our romantic partners.

3. **Mirror Neuron System**: This network of brain cells activates both when we perform an action and when we observe someone else performing that action. It helps us understand others' experiences by creating a kind of internal simulation of what they might be feeling.

Dr. Helen Riess, a psychiatrist at Harvard Medical School, explains that these neural systems allow us to "try on" our partner's emotional experience. When functioning optimally, they create what neuroscientists call "neural resonance" – a state where our brain activity actually begins to synchronize with our partner's during moments of deep understanding.

What's particularly fascinating is that these neural systems can be strengthened through practice. Dr. Richard

Davidson's research at the University of Wisconsin-Madison has shown that regular perspective-taking exercises actually increase neural connectivity in these regions, making understanding others more automatic and accurate over time.

Attachment Theory and Understanding

Dr. Sue Johnson, explains that these attachment patterns significantly influence our ability to understand our partners. People with secure attachment histories typically find it easier to consider alternative perspectives without feeling threatened. Those with anxious attachment patterns may be hypervigilant to signs of rejection but sometimes misinterpret neutral cues as negative. Those with avoidant patterns may disengage from deeper understanding as a self-protective measure.

The Four Dimensions of Understanding

To truly understand your partner, you need to develop awareness across four key dimensions:

1. **Cognitive Understanding**: Comprehending how your partner thinks, processes information, and makes decisions. Some people are analytical and logical, while others are more intuitive. Some need to process information slowly and thoroughly, while others make quick decisions based on limited data.

2. **Emotional Understanding**: Recognizing and validating your partner's emotional landscape—what triggers certain feelings, how they express emotions, and what they need when experiencing different emotional states.

3. **Historical Understanding**: Appreciating how your partner's past experiences— their family dynamics, previous relationships, cultural background, and formative events—shape their current perceptions and reactions.

4. **Needs-Based Understanding**: Identifying your partner's core psychological needs —for security, autonomy, connection, validation, etc.—and how these needs influence their behavior and desires.

Dialogue Example: The Four Dimensions in Action

Partner A: "I don't understand why you got so upset when my parents called and said they wanted to visit this weekend. They're just trying to be close to us."

Partner B: "I know it seems like I overreacted, but let me try to explain where I'm coming from..."

Cognitive Dimension: *"When sudden changes of plans happen, my brain goes into overdrive trying to reorganize everything. Unlike you, I need time to mentally prepare for social interactions, even with family."*

Emotional Dimension: "*I felt anxious and overwhelmed because I already had a stressful week planned, and the thought of hosting guests—even people I care about—felt like too much.*"

Historical Dimension: "*Growing up, my parents never respected my boundaries around time and space. They would make demands and expect immediate compliance. When your parents called with such short notice, it triggered those old feelings of having my boundaries violated.*"

Needs-Based Dimension: "*I have a strong need for autonomy and the ability to control my environment and schedule. When that's threatened, I feel destabilized and defensive.*"

Partner A: "I had no idea all of that was happening for you. I thought you were just being difficult about my parents. Now I understand why you reacted that way, and it makes perfect sense given your experience."

This example illustrates how exploring all four dimensions can transform a potential conflict into an opportunity for deeper understanding and connection.

Mentalization: The Science of Understanding Others

Psychologists Peter Fonagy and Anthony Bateman have developed a concept called "mentalization" – the ability to understand the mental state of oneself and others. Their research shows that this capacity develops in early childhood through secure attachment relationships and continues to evolve throughout life.

Mentalization involves recognizing that:

1. We all have minds that are opaque to direct observation

2. Mental states (thoughts, feelings, needs) drive behavior

3. Our perceptions are interpretations, not facts

4. Understanding others requires active inquiry, not assumption

Dr. Fonagy's research has shown that couples with strong mentalization abilities demonstrate greater relationship resilience, particularly during conflict. They're able to maintain what he calls "epistemic trust" – the ability to continue seeing their partner as a reliable source of information even during disagreements.

What's particularly encouraging about mentalization research is that this capacity can be developed at any age. Through specific practices that promote curiosity about mental states, couples can significantly improve their understanding of each other, even after years of misunderstanding.

Barriers to Understanding: What Gets in Our Way

Even with the best intentions, several common obstacles can prevent us from truly understanding our partners:

1. **Defensive Listening**: When we feel criticized or threatened, we often stop listening to understand and start listening to defend ourselves. Our focus shifts from our partner's perspective to formulating our rebuttal.

2. **Confirmation Bias**: We tend to notice and remember information that confirms our existing beliefs about our partner while filtering out contradictory evidence.

3. **Mind Reading**: Assuming we know what our partner is thinking or feeling without actually checking with them.

4. **Emotional Flooding**: When strong emotions like anger or hurt overwhelm us, our cognitive abilities—including perspective-taking—become significantly impaired.

5. **Fundamental Attribution Error**: The tendency to attribute our own behavior to situational factors ("I snapped because I had a terrible day") while attributing our partner's behavior to character flaws ("You snapped because you're impatient and inconsiderate").

From a neurobiological perspective, these barriers make perfect sense. When we feel threatened, the brain's amygdala activates, triggering what neuroscientists call the "fight-flight-freeze" response. This survival mechanism evolved to protect us from physical threats, but it also activates during emotional threats, including relationship conflicts.

When the amygdala is highly activated, it actually inhibits activity in the prefrontal cortex – the very brain region we need for perspective-taking and empathic understanding. Dr. Daniel Siegel calls this process "flipping our lid" – when our higher cognitive functions become temporarily unavailable due to emotional arousal.

Understanding this neurobiological process helps explain why it's so difficult to see our partner's perspective when we're upset. It's not just a matter of willpower – our brains are literally in a state that makes understanding more difficult.

Exercise: Developing Your Understanding Skills
Exercise 1: Perspective-Taking Practice
Time needed: 20-30 minutes **Materials:** Paper and pen for each person
Choose a recent disagreement or misunderstanding that wasn't too emotionally charged. Take turns writing down your perspective of what happened, including:
- What you were thinking

- What you were feeling

- What you needed or wanted

- What you believed your partner was thinking/feeling/needing

Then exchange papers and read each other's perspectives without interruption or debate. Afterward, discuss what surprised you about your partner's perspective and what you learned.

Exercise: The Understanding Interview
Time needed: 30-45 minutes **Materials:** None
Take turns interviewing each other about a topic where you have different viewpoints or preferences. The interviewer's job is solely to understand, not to convince or respond with their own perspective. Ask questions like:

- "What experiences shaped your view on this?"

- "What values or principles guide your thinking here?"

- "What concerns or fears do you have about the alternative approach?"

- "What needs are you trying to meet with this preference?"

After each interview, the listener summarizes what they heard to confirm understanding.

Understanding Across Difference: Bridging Significant Gaps

Some of the most challenging understanding gaps occur across significant differences in background, identity, or experience. These might include differences in:

- Cultural or religious background
- Gender socialization
- Socioeconomic upbringing
- Neurodiversity (e.g., one partner is neurotypical while the other has ADHD, autism, etc.)
- Trauma history

Case Study: Cultural Understanding

Mei, who grew up in a traditional Chinese family, and David, who was raised in a progressive American household, struggled with understanding each other's approaches to family involvement in their relationship.

David couldn't understand why Mei consulted her parents before making major decisions that he felt should be between just the two of them. From his perspective, this indicated a lack of independence and autonomy in their relationship.

Mei, meanwhile, was hurt by what she perceived as David's disrespect toward her family bonds. In her cultural context, family interdependence was a sign of respect and love, not a lack of autonomy.

Their breakthrough came when they stopped trying to convince each other that their approach was "right" and instead focused on understanding the cultural values and experiences that shaped each perspective. David learned about the concept of filial piety in Chinese culture, while Mei gained insight into the high value placed on individual autonomy in David's upbringing.

This deeper understanding didn't eliminate their differences, but it transformed them from a source of conflict to an opportunity for growth. They were able to create a hybrid approach that honored both sets of values—consulting family for guidance while maintaining their autonomy as the final decision-makers.

When bridging significant differences, remember these principles:

1. **Approach with Curiosity, Not Judgment**: Assume that your partner's perspective makes sense given their experiences, even if it seems foreign to you.

2. **Acknowledge the Validity of Different Realities**:

Different doesn't mean wrong— two contradictory experiences can both be valid.

3. **Look for the Underlying Needs and Values**: Often, seemingly opposite behaviors are attempts to meet similar fundamental needs, just expressed differently.

4. **Be Willing to Be Wrong About Your Assumptions**: Some of our most deeply held beliefs about "how things should be" are actually culturally or personally conditioned, not universal truths.

Understanding as an Ongoing Practice

Understanding isn't a destination—it's an ongoing journey. Even couples who have been together for decades continue to discover new aspects of each other. People grow and change, and so must our understanding of them.

The goal isn't perfect understanding (which is impossible) but rather a commitment to the practice of trying to understand—to approaching your partner with curiosity rather than assumption, with openness rather than certainty.

This commitment to understanding creates a relationship environment where both partners feel seen, valued, and respected in their uniqueness. It transforms differences from sources of conflict into opportunities for growth and deeper connection.

Dialogue Scripts: Understanding in Action

Here are some examples of language that facilitates understanding:

When your partner shares something you find confusing: "That's different from how I might see it, which makes me really curious to understand more about your perspective. Could you help me see this through your eyes?"

When you notice your partner seems upset: "I can see something's bothering you, and I want to understand what you're experiencing. Would you be willing to share what's going on for you right now?"

When you realize you've misunderstood: "I think I've been making assumptions about what you need in this situation. I'd like to step back and really listen to what would actually be helpful for you."

When bridging a significant difference: "We seem to have very different approaches to this. I'm guessing we both have good reasons for our perspectives. Could we each share the experiences or values that shape how we see this?"

Chapter Reflection: Your Understanding Patterns

Take a moment to reflect on your current understanding patterns in your relationship:

    1. In what areas do you feel most understood by your

partner? Least understood?

2. What aspects of your partner's perspective do you find most challenging to understand or relate to?

3. What assumptions do you make about your partner's thoughts, feelings, or motivations that might benefit from verification?

4. How might your own background, experiences, or personality be creating filters through which you interpret your partner's behavior?

5. What's one area where you could commit to deepening your understanding of your partner this week?

The Bridge to the Next Element: From Understanding to Listening

Understanding and listening are intimately connected elements of the P.U.L.S.E. framework. While understanding is about the cognitive and emotional process of seeing through your partner's eyes, listening is about the behavioral skills that make understanding possible.

In the next chapter, we'll explore how to develop listening skills that go beyond simply hearing words to truly receiving your partner's experience. You'll learn practical approaches to what communication researchers call "active listening"—the ability to be fully present, engaged, and responsive to your partner's communication.

But before we move on, I encourage you to begin implementing at least one understanding practice from this chapter. Remember that neural pathways strengthen through consistent activation—each effort to see through your partner's eyes literally reshapes your brain's empathy circuits, gradually creating a relationship where differences become opportunities for connection rather than sources of conflict.

LOVE WITH P.U.L.S.E.

KEEP GOING AFTER THE CHAPTER ENDS

- Guided Video Exercises
- Printable Worksheets
- Real-Life Tools You Can Use Today

Turn what you just read into what you can actually do — right now.

Dr. Ashley R. Bryant

Creator of the P.U.L.S.E. Framework & Author of Love With P.U.L.S.E.

Already finished the book? Scan to access every chapter's bonus content in one place.

Chapter 4
Listen: The Art of Hearing Hearts, Not Just Words

Have you ever had the experience of talking to your partner and feeling like your words are simply bouncing off an invisible wall? Or perhaps you've been on the receiving end of that frustrated look that says, "You're not really hearing me, are you?" If so, you're not alone. Despite communication being fundamental to human connection, truly effective listening is surprisingly rare—especially in our closest relationships.

In this chapter, we'll explore the third element of the P.U.L.S.E. framework: Listen. We'll discover why listening is so much more than simply hearing words, how to overcome common barriers to deep listening, and how to develop this transformative skill in your relationship.

The Listening Crisis in Modern Relationships

In today's hyper-connected yet paradoxically disconnected world, we face what I call a "listening crisis." We're constantly bombarded with information, notifications, and distractions that fragment our attention and diminish our capacity for deep, focused listening. The average person now has an attention span shorter than that of a goldfish— about eight seconds, according to some studies.

This crisis manifests acutely in our intimate relationships. Partners report feeling unheard, misunderstood, and invalidated, even when they spend hours "talking" to each other. The problem isn't necessarily a lack of time spent communicating; it's the quality of that communication—specifically, the quality of our listening.

Case Study: The Dinner Table Disconnect

Jason and Emma sat across from each other at their favorite restaurant, ostensibly enjoying a date night. But the scene was all too familiar: Emma was sharing a story about a conflict with her colleague, while Jason nodded occasionally, his eyes darting to his phone every few minutes to check scores from the game.

"So anyway," Emma continued, "I felt completely undermined in the meeting, and I'm not sure how to address it tomorrow..."

Jason looked up. "Hmm? Oh, yeah, that's tough. You should just tell her how you feel."

Emma's face fell. "I just spent five minutes explaining why that wouldn't work in this situation. Were you even listening?"

Jason felt defensive. "Of course I was! You were talking about that problem with Sarah at work."

"Her name is Stephanie, and that's not even the point..."

This exchange captures a common dynamic: one partner feels unheard and invalidated, while the other feels unfairly accused of not listening when they believe they were. The truth is, Jason was hearing Emma's words, but he wasn't truly listening—not with the depth and presence that creates genuine connection.

The Science of Listening: Why It Matters So Profoundly

Research in relationship psychology reveals that effective listening is one of the strongest predictors of relationship satisfaction and longevity. When partners feel truly heard, they report higher levels of emotional intimacy, trust, and overall happiness in the relationship.

Neurologically, being deeply listened to activates the brain's reward centers, releasing dopamine and oxytocin—chemicals associated with pleasure, bonding, and trust. Conversely, feeling unheard or dismissed activates the brain's threat response, triggering stress hormones like cortisol and adrenaline.

This biological response explains why poor listening can escalate conflicts so quickly. When we don't feel heard, we don't just feel frustrated—we feel threatened at a primal level. Our brain interprets the lack of attentive listening as rejection or dismissal, triggering defensive reactions that further impair communication.

The Neuroscience of Deep Listening

Recent advances in neuroscience have given us remarkable insights into what happens in the brain during different types of listening. When we engage in deep, attentive listening, several important neural processes occur:

1. **Neural Synchrony**: Research by Dr. Uri Hasson at Princeton University has shown that during effective communication, the listener's brain activity actually begins to synchronize with the speaker's. Using functional MRI, Hasson's team observed that when someone is truly engaged in listening, their neural patterns start to mirror those of the person speaking. This "brain-to-brain coupling" creates what neuroscientists call "neural resonance" – a state where two people's brains are literally "on the same wavelength."

2. **Default Mode Network Activation**: The brain's default mode network – regions associated with empathy, self-referential thought, and social cognition – becomes highly active during deep listening. Dr. Matthew Lieberman's research at UCLA shows that this network helps us understand others' mental states and experiences, creating the foundation for empathic connection.

3. **Inhibition of Self-Focus**: Studies using EEG (electroencephalography) reveal that effective

listening involves temporarily dampening activity in brain regions associated with self-reference and self-focus. This neural inhibition allows us to truly center our attention on our partner rather than ourselves.

4. **Stress Regulation Effects**: Dr. James Coan's research on the neurobiology of emotional support demonstrates that feeling truly heard and understood actually reduces activity in the brain's threat-detection systems, particularly the amygdala. This creates what neuroscientists call a "social buffering effect" – the presence of an attentive, supportive listener literally helps regulate our nervous system during stress.

What's particularly fascinating is that these neural processes don't just affect the moment of communication – they create lasting changes in relationship quality. Dr. John Gottman's research at the University of Washington has shown that couples who regularly engage in attentive listening show different patterns of physiological regulation during conflict, with lower heart rates, blood pressure, and stress hormone levels compared to couples with poor listening habits.

The Four Levels of Listening

Not all listening is created equal. In my work with couples, I've identified four distinct levels of listening, each with progressively deeper impact:

1. **Dismissive Listening**: This is barely listening at all. The listener is physically present but mentally elsewhere—checking their phone, watching TV, or simply waiting for their turn to speak. They might offer token responses like "uh-huh" or "that's nice," but there's no real engagement.

2. **Factual Listening**: At this level, the listener is paying enough attention to absorb basic facts and information. They could repeat back the general content of what was said, but they're missing emotional nuances and deeper meanings. This is the "just the facts" approach.

3. **Empathic Listening**: Here, the listener is tuned in not just to words but to emotions and unspoken messages. They're actively trying to understand both the content and the feelings behind what's being shared. They notice tone, facial expressions, and body language.

4. **Transformative Listening**: This highest level involves complete presence and openness. The listener temporarily sets aside their own perspective to fully enter the speaker's world. They listen without judgment, without planning their response, and without trying to fix or solve. This type of listening creates a space where both people can be transformed by the exchange.

Most relationship conflicts involve partners operating at different listening levels. One person might be seeking empathic or transformative listening while the other is providing factual listening at best. This mismatch creates frustration and disconnection.

Dialogue Example: The Four Levels in Action

Partner: "I had such a frustrating day at work. My boss completely changed the project requirements at the last minute, and now I have to redo everything by tomorrow."

Dismissive Response: "Mmm-hmm..." (while scrolling through social media)

Factual Response: "So your boss changed the requirements and gave you a tight deadline. That's work for you."

Empathic Response: "That sounds incredibly frustrating. You put all that work in, and now you have to start over with no extra time. You must be feeling really overwhelmed right now."

Transformative Response: "I can hear how frustrated and pressured you feel. This seems to be hitting on that value you have about respect for people's time and effort. Would it help to talk through how you're planning to approach this, or do you just need space to vent about it right now?"

The difference in how these responses would make the speaker feel is profound. The dismissive response leaves them feeling invisible, the factual response acknowledged but not understood, the empathic response validated, and the transformative response deeply seen and supported.

Co-Regulation Through Listening

One of the most fascinating discoveries in interpersonal neurobiology is the concept of "co-regulation" – the process by which one person's nervous system can help regulate another's. Dr. Stephen Porges, developer of Polyvagal Theory, explains that humans have evolved to use social connection as a primary method of regulating our physiological states.

When we feel truly heard and understood, our nervous system receives powerful cues of safety that activate what Porges calls the "ventral vagal complex" – the part of our parasympathetic nervous system associated with calm, connection, and social engagement. This physiological shift has profound effects on our emotional state, cognitive function, and even immune system.

Research using measures of heart rate variability (HRV) – a key indicator of nervous system regulation – shows that during moments of attentive listening between partners, their heart rhythms actually begin to synchronize. This physiological attunement creates what researchers call "interpersonal biobehavioral synchrony" – a state where two people's biological rhythms become coordinated.

This science helps explain why being truly listened to can feel so profoundly calming and healing, while feeling unheard can trigger such intense distress. When our partner listens attentively, they're not just gathering information – they're literally helping regulate our nervous system.

Barriers to Deep Listening: What Gets in Our Way

Even with the best intentions, several common obstacles can prevent us from listening deeply to our partners:

1. **Digital Distractions**: Perhaps the most obvious modern barrier—our devices constantly compete for our attention, making it difficult to be fully present.

2. **The Problem-Solving Reflex**: Especially common among men (though certainly not exclusive to them), the instinct to immediately offer solutions rather than simply listening and validating can short-circuit meaningful connection.

3. **Self-Referential Listening**: This happens when we filter everything our partner says through our own experiences—"That reminds me of when I..." or "I know exactly how you feel because..."—shifting the focus back to ourselves.

4. **Defensive Listening**: When we perceive criticism or blame (whether it's actually there or not), we often stop listening to understand and start listening to defend ourselves.

5. **Assumption of Mind-Reading**: The belief that "if they really loved me, they would know what I need without me having to say it" creates unrealistic expectations and prevents clear communication.

6. **Emotional Flooding**: When we're overwhelmed by strong emotions, our capacity to listen effectively diminishes dramatically. Our brain's limbic system (emotional center) overrides our prefrontal cortex (rational thinking), making deep listening nearly impossible.

From a neurobiological perspective, these barriers make perfect sense. When we feel threatened or overwhelmed, the brain's executive function networks – regions responsible for attention, perspective-taking, and impulse control – become less active. Dr. Daniel Siegel calls this process "flipping our lid" – when our higher cognitive functions become temporarily unavailable due to emotional arousal.

Understanding this neurobiological process helps explain why it's so difficult to listen well when we're upset. It's not just a matter of willpower – our brains are literally in a state that makes attentive listening more difficult.

Practical Exercises: Developing Your Listening Skills

Exercise: The Speaker-Listener Technique
Time needed: 20-30 minutes **Materials:** A timer, a small object to serve as a "talking token"

This structured exercise helps couples practice focused listening without interruption:

1. Choose a topic to discuss—something meaningful but not your most volatile issue.

2. Decide who will speak first. This person holds the "talking token" (any small object).

3. The speaker shares their thoughts and feelings on the topic for 3-5 minutes, using "I" statements.

4. The listener may not interrupt. Their only job is to listen attentively.

5. When the speaker finishes, the listener summarizes what they heard, focusing on both content and emotions: "What I heard you saying is..."

6. The speaker confirms or clarifies: "Yes, that's it" or "What I meant was..."

7. Switch roles and repeat.

This exercise helps break the pattern of interrupting and teaches the skill of listening to understand rather than to respond.

Exercise: Mindful Listening Practice
Time needed: 10 minutes daily **Materials:** None

For one week, commit to practicing mindful listening during a daily check-in:

1. Set aside 10 minutes when you're both relatively relaxed.

2. Remove all distractions—phones, TV, computers.

3. Sit facing each other.

4. Take three deep breaths together to center yourselves.

5. Take turns sharing about your day, focusing especially on emotional experiences.

6. When listening, practice full presence—maintain eye contact, notice your partner's facial expressions and body language, and resist the urge to plan your response.

7. After each person shares, the listener reflects back one thing they appreciated about how their partner expressed themselves.

This brief daily practice builds the muscle of attentive listening and creates a ritual of connection.

Listening in Difficult Moments: When It Matters Most (And Is Hardest)

The true test of listening skills comes during conflict or emotional distress—precisely when effective listening is most challenging yet most crucial. Here are strategies for listening well during difficult conversations:

1. **Recognize Your Triggers**: Learn to identify when you're shifting from open listening to defensive or dismissive listening. Physical cues might include tension in your jaw or chest, holding your breath, or an urge to interrupt.

2. **Use the Pause Button**: When you notice yourself becoming reactive, take a deliberate pause. A simple "I want to make sure I understand you fully. Can I take a moment to process what you're saying?" gives you space to reset.

3. **Validate Before Responding**: Even if you disagree with your partner's perspective, validate their feelings first: "I can see why you'd feel that way" or "That makes sense from your perspective."

4. **Ask Clarifying Questions**: Instead of making assumptions, ask: "Can you help me understand more about why this is so important to you?" or "What would be most helpful from me right now?"

5. **Monitor Your Body Language**: Communication is mostly nonverbal. Maintain an open posture, appropriate eye contact, and nodding to show engagement.

Case Study: Listening Through Conflict

Rachel and Miguel were discussing their different approaches to parenting their teenage son. Rachel felt Miguel was too lenient, while Miguel thought Rachel was too strict. Their conversations on this topic typically devolved into accusations and defensiveness.

During a therapy session, they learned to implement a structured listening approach. When discussing their son's curfew, instead of immediately arguing for their position, each took turns fully expressing their concerns while the other practiced deep listening.

Rachel shared her fear that without clear boundaries, their son might make dangerous choices. Miguel listened without interrupting, then reflected: "I hear that your strictness comes from a place of deep love and concern for his safety. You're afraid that without firm rules, he could get hurt."

When it was Miguel's turn, he expressed his worry that too many restrictions would push their son to rebel and hide things from them. Rachel listened attentively, then reflected: "I understand that you're concerned about maintaining open communication with him, and you fear that being too strict might damage that trust."

This exchange didn't immediately resolve their different parenting approaches, but it transformed the nature of their discussion from adversarial to collaborative. By truly hearing *the fears and values underlying each other's positions, they could begin working toward a solution that addressed both sets of concerns.*

Gender Differences in Listening: Navigating Different Styles

Research suggests that men and women often have different listening styles and needs, though these are generalizations and don't apply to everyone. Understanding these potential differences can help partners bridge communication gaps:

Common patterns in male listening:

- More solution-oriented; tendency to listen for problems to solve

- May process emotions internally rather than through verbal expression

- Often prefer side-by-side communication (while doing an activity) to face to-face

- May need time to process before responding to emotional topics

Common patterns in female listening:

- More relationally oriented; tendency to listen for emotional connection

- Often process emotions through verbal expression

- Typically prefer face-to-face communication with eye contact

- May use listening as a way to build rapport and solidarity

These differences aren't inherently problematic, but they can create misunderstandings when partners have different expectations about what constitutes good listening. The key is to understand and respect these differences rather than judging them.

For example, when a woman shares a problem, she may primarily be seeking empathy and connection, while her male partner might assume she wants solutions. Neither approach is wrong—they're just different listening styles serving different needs.

Dialogue Scripts: Effective Listening in Action

Here are some examples of language that facilitates deep listening in different relationship contexts:

When your partner is sharing something difficult: "I want to make sure I really understand what you're experiencing. Can you tell me more about how this is affecting you? I'm here to listen, not to fix or judge."

When you're having trouble staying present: "I notice I'm feeling distracted right now, and what you're sharing is important to me. Can we pause for a moment so I can refocus my attention fully on you?"

When you want to check your understanding: "I want to make sure I'm really getting what you're saying. What I hear you expressing is [summarize content and emotions]. Is that accurate, or have I missed something important?"

When responding to vulnerability: "Thank you for trusting me with this. It means a lot that you feel safe enough to share such personal feelings with me. I'm here with you in this."

When you disagree but want to listen first: "I have a different perspective on this, but right now I really want to understand your view fully before I share mine. Can you tell me more about how you came to see it this way?"

Chapter Reflection: Your Listening Journey

Take a moment to reflect on listening in your relationship:

1. What level of listening (dismissive, factual, empathic, or transformative) do you most commonly practice with your partner? What about them with you?

2. What are your biggest barriers to deep listening? What specific situations or topics make it most difficult for you to stay present and attentive?

3. How were listening skills modeled (or not modeled) in your family of origin? How might this influence your current listening patterns?

4. What difference would it make in your relationship if both you and your partner consistently practiced deeper levels of listening?

5. Which listening practice from this chapter seems most relevant to enhancing your specific relationship right now?

The Bridge to the Next Element: From Listening to Self-Regulation

While effective listening creates the foundation for understanding and connection, it requires another crucial skill: self-regulation. In the next chapter, we'll explore how managing your own emotional responses—particularly during challenging interactions —creates the internal stability needed for all other relationship skills to flourish.

We'll discover how developing greater emotional awareness and regulation helps you stay present during difficult conversations, respond thoughtfully rather than reactively, and create the kind of emotional safety that allows vulnerability to flourish. You'll learn practical approaches to what psychologists call "emotional intelligence"—the ability to recognize, understand, and manage your own emotions while responding sensitively to your partner's.

But before we move on, I encourage you to begin implementing at least one listening practice from this chapter. Remember that neural pathways strengthen through consistent activation—each effort to listen deeply literally reshapes your brain's communication patterns, gradually creating a relationship where both partners feel truly heard and understood.

LOVE WITH P.U.L.S.E.

KEEP GOING AFTER THE CHAPTER ENDS

- Guided Video Exercises
- Printable Worksheets
- Real-Life Tools You Can Use Today

Turn what you just read into what you can actually do — right now.

Dr. Ashley R. Bryant

Creator of the P.U.L.S.E. Framework & Author of Love With P.U.L.S.E.

Already finished the book? Scan to access every chapter's bonus content in one place.

Chapter 5

Self-Regulate: Mastering Your Inner Storms to Create Outer Calm

Have you ever said something in the heat of an argument that you immediately regretted? Or perhaps you've shut down completely during a difficult conversation, unable to articulate your thoughts or feelings? Maybe you've found yourself overreacting to a minor comment from your partner, unleashing a disproportionate emotional response that left both of you confused and hurt?

If you're nodding in recognition, you're experiencing what happens when our emotional regulation systems are overwhelmed—when our inner storms take control, often with consequences for our most important relationships. This chapter explores the fourth element of the P.U.L.S.E. framework: Self-regulation, the essential skill of managing your emotional responses, especially during challenging interactions with your partner.

The Emotional Brain in Relationships

To understand self-regulation, we first need to understand how our brains process emotions, particularly in intimate relationships. Our brains have evolved with three primary sections that work together—though not always harmoniously:

1. **The Reptilian Brain (Brainstem)**: The oldest part of our brain, responsible for basic survival functions and instinctive reactions like fight, flight, freeze, or fawn.

2. **The Limbic System (Emotional Brain)**: This processes emotions and stores emotional memories. It includes the amygdala, which acts as our brain's alarm system, and the hippocampus, which helps form memories.

3. **The Neocortex (Thinking Brain)**: The newest part of our brain, responsible for rational thought, planning, problem-solving, and empathy.

When we're calm and feeling safe, these three parts work together beautifully. Our thinking brain stays online, allowing us to respond thoughtfully to situations. But when we perceive a threat—whether physical or emotional—our limbic system can hijack the process, triggering a cascade of stress hormones that prepare us for survival and temporarily bypass our rational thinking.

This is where relationship conflicts often go awry. When we feel criticized, dismissed, or threatened by our partner (even unintentionally), our brain can react as if we're facing a physical threat. Blood flow decreases to our neocortex, making it literally harder to think clearly, access empathy, or communicate effectively. We might lash out with harsh words, withdraw into stony silence, or engage in other behaviors that damage connection.

The Neuroscience of Self-Regulation

Recent advances in neuroscience have given us remarkable insights into what happens in the brain during emotional regulation and dysregulation. Dr. Stephen Porges' Polyvagal Theory provides a comprehensive framework for understanding the neurobiological basis of our emotional responses in relationships.

According to Porges, our autonomic nervous system has three distinct branches that evolved over time:

1. **The Ventral Vagal Complex (VVC)**: The newest branch, associated with social engagement, connection, and calm states. When this system is activated, we can think clearly, communicate effectively, and maintain emotional balance.

2. **The Sympathetic Nervous System (SNS)**: The mobilization system that triggers our "fight or flight" response. When activated, it increases heart rate, releases stress hormones like adrenaline and cortisol, and prepares the body for action.

3. **The Dorsal Vagal Complex (DVC)**: The oldest branch,

responsible for the "freeze" or shutdown response. When activated, it can cause immobilization, dissociation, or emotional numbing.

Dr. Porges explains that these systems operate in a hierarchical manner. When we feel safe, our ventral vagal system dominates, allowing us to connect and communicate effectively. When we perceive threat, our nervous system shifts to sympathetic activation (fight/flight) or, in cases of overwhelming threat, to dorsal vagal shutdown (freeze).

Neuroimaging studies by Dr. Kevin Ochsner at Columbia University have revealed the specific brain regions involved in emotional regulation. When we successfully regulate our emotions, we see increased activity in the prefrontal cortex (particularly the ventromedial and dorsolateral regions) and decreased activity in the amygdala. This prefrontal-amygdala connection is crucial for emotional balance.

What's particularly encouraging about this research is that these neural pathways can be strengthened through practice. Dr. Richard Davidson's work at the University of Wisconsin-Madison has shown that regular emotional regulation practices actually change brain structure and function over time, increasing the density of neural connections between regulatory regions and emotional centers.

Case Study: The Emotional Hijacking

Alex and Jordan were getting ready for a dinner party with Alex's colleagues. As they were about to leave, Jordan noticed a stain on Alex's shirt and pointed it out. What happened next surprised them both: Alex exploded with anger, accusing Jordan of always finding fault and trying to control everything. Jordan was stunned by the intensity of the reaction to what seemed like a helpful comment.

Later, when they processed what happened, Alex realized the reaction wasn't really about the shirt at all. Growing up with a hypercritical parent who would inspect Alex before any social event and find something to criticize, the simple comment about the shirt had triggered old feelings of inadequacy and shame. Alex's emotional brain had connected Jordan's innocent remark to painful childhood experiences, bypassing rational thought and triggering a defensive outburst.

This is a classic example of emotional hijacking—when our limbic system takes over, causing us to react from old wounds rather than responding to the present reality.

Attachment Theory and Emotional Regulation

People with secure attachment histories typically develop more robust self-regulation capacities because they experienced consistent co-regulation from caregivers. Those with anxious attachment patterns may become quickly flooded with emotion during relationship conflicts, while those with avoidant patterns may suppress or disconnect from emotions as a self-protective strategy.

Research by Dr. James Gross at Stanford University has identified two primary strategies people use for emotional regulation:

1. **Antecedent-focused strategies**: These occur before the emotional response is fully activated, such as situation selection (avoiding triggering situations), attention deployment (focusing on different aspects of a situation), and cognitive reappraisal (changing how we think about a situation).

2. **Response-focused strategies**: These occur after the emotion is already activated, such as suppression (hiding emotional expression) or various coping behaviors.

Interestingly, research shows that antecedent-focused strategies, particularly cognitive reappraisal, are generally more effective and less physiologically taxing than response focused strategies like suppression. This explains why learning to recognize early warning signs of emotional activation and intervening quickly is so valuable in relationship contexts.

The Self-Regulation Paradox: Why It's So Hard (Yet So Important)

Here's the paradox of self-regulation in relationships: It's most crucial precisely when it's most difficult. When we're triggered, flooded with stress hormones, and our thinking brain is going offline, that's exactly when we most need to access our self-regulation skills—yet that's when these skills are hardest to access.

This explains why couples often find themselves caught in destructive patterns despite their best intentions. It's not that they don't know better or don't care; it's that in moments of emotional flooding, their capacity for thoughtful response is biologically compromised.

The good news is that self-regulation is a skill that can be developed with practice. By understanding your triggers, recognizing the early signs of emotional flooding, and implementing specific strategies, you can learn to navigate even intense emotions without damaging your connection.

The Science of Emotional Co-Regulation

Interestingly, research in neuroscience and attachment theory reveals that humans aren't designed to regulate their emotions entirely on their own. We're wired for co regulation—the process by which one person's regulated nervous system helps calm another's. This begins in infancy, as caregivers soothe distressed babies, and continues throughout our lives in close relationships.

In healthy adult relationships, partners help regulate each other's emotional states through presence, touch, tone of voice, and empathic response. When one partner is dysregulated, the other's calm presence can help restore balance. This is why having a secure attachment with your partner creates a foundation for better emotional regulation.

However, this co-regulation system can also work in reverse. When both partners become dysregulated, they can amplify each other's stress responses, creating an escalating cycle of reactivity. This is why learning individual self-regulation skills is so important—it allows you to break this cycle and offer co-regulation to your partner even during difficult moments.

Recognizing Your Personal Triggers and Response Patterns

The first step in developing better self-regulation is self-awareness—understanding your unique triggers and how you typically respond when emotionally activated.

Common Relationship Triggers

While triggers are highly individual, some common relationship triggers include:

- Feeling criticized or judged
- Sensing rejection or abandonment
- Perceiving control or manipulation
- Feeling disrespected or dismissed Experiencing

unfairness or injustice

- Sensing a threat to autonomy or independence
- Feeling inadequate or like a failure

Response Patterns: The Four F's

When triggered, most people default to one or more of these response patterns:

1. **Fight**: Becoming argumentative, critical, or aggressive; raising your voice; using harsh language or accusations.

2. **Flight**: Physically or emotionally withdrawing; changing the subject; becoming busy with other tasks; emotionally checking out.

3. **Freeze**: Becoming silent or immobilized; feeling unable to think or speak; "deer in headlights" response.

4. **Fawn**: People-pleasing; abandoning your own needs or perspective to appease; excessive apologizing.

Exercise: Mapping Your Emotional Landscape
Time needed: 30-45 minutes **Materials:** Journal or paper, pen
Take time to reflect on and write about these questions:
1. What are your top three emotional triggers in your

relationship? Be specific about situations, words, or behaviors that consistently activate your stress response.

2. How do you typically know you're becoming triggered? What physical sensations, thoughts, or behavioral changes do you notice? (Examples: tight chest, racing thoughts, clenched jaw, desire to leave)

3. Which of the four F's (fight, flight, freeze, fawn) is your default response pattern? Do you have different patterns in different situations?

4. Can you trace any of your triggers to past experiences or relationship patterns? How might understanding these origins help you respond differently?

5. What helps you return to a regulated state after becoming triggered? What self soothing strategies have worked for you?

Share your insights with your partner if you feel comfortable, and invite them to share theirs. This mutual understanding can help both of you recognize and respond more compassionately to each other's emotional patterns.

The Window of Tolerance: Your Emotional Sweet Spot

A helpful concept in understanding self-regulation is the "window of tolerance," developed by psychiatrist Dr. Dan Siegel. This refers to the optimal zone of arousal where you can function effectively—where you're neither too activated (anxious, angry, panicked) nor too deactivated (numb, disconnected, shut down).

When you're within your window of tolerance, you can: - Think clearly and rationally - Feel emotions without being overwhelmed by them - Connect with others empathically - Respond flexibly to situations - Access your values and intentions

When you're outside your window of tolerance—either hyperaroused (too activated) or hypoaroused (too deactivated)—your ability to communicate effectively and connect with your partner is compromised.

The goal of self-regulation isn't to never feel intense emotions; it's to expand your window of tolerance so you can experience a wider range of emotions while still maintaining your capacity for thoughtful response and connection.

Dialogue Example: Discussing Windows of Tolerance

Partner A: "I've noticed that when we discuss finances, I tend to get really anxious and start talking really fast, interrupting

you. I think I'm going outside my window of tolerance into hyperarousal."

Partner B: "That makes sense. And I think I do the opposite—I get overwhelmed and shut down, probably going into hypoarousal. No wonder these conversations are so difficult."

Partner A: "What if we tried to recognize these patterns in the moment? Maybe we could have a signal or word to indicate when one of us is starting to go outside our window?"

Partner B: "I like that idea. And maybe we could agree to take a short break when that happens, just to regulate ourselves, before continuing the conversation."

Practical Strategies for Self-Regulation

Now that we understand the importance of self-regulation and how to recognize when we're becoming dysregulated, let's explore specific strategies for returning to our window of tolerance during challenging relationship moments.

1. Physiological Regulation: Calming Your Body

Since emotional dysregulation has powerful physical components, addressing the body's stress response is often the most direct path to regaining balance:

Deep Breathing: The simplest yet most effective tool. Practice 4-7-8 breathing: inhale for 4 counts, hold for 7, exhale for 8. This activates your parasympathetic nervous system, counteracting the stress response.

Progressive Muscle Relaxation: Systematically tense and release muscle groups throughout your body, releasing physical tension that accompanies emotional stress.

Cold Exposure: Splash cold water on your face or place an ice pack on your forehead. This triggers the mammalian dive reflex, which slows heart rate and reduces emotional intensity.

Physical Movement: If appropriate, excuse yourself for a brief walk or stretch. Movement helps process stress hormones and shift your physiological state.

Research by Dr. Bessel van der Kolk, a leading trauma researcher, has shown that these body-based approaches are particularly effective because they directly address the physiological aspects of emotional dysregulation. His work demonstrates that "the body keeps the score" – emotional distress is stored physically, and therefore physical interventions can be powerful regulatory tools.

Dr. Stephen Porges explains that these physiological strategies work by activating the vagus nerve, which is the primary nerve of the parasympathetic nervous system. When stimulated through deep breathing, cold exposure, or certain forms of movement, the vagus nerve sends signals throughout the body to lower heart rate, reduce blood pressure, and decrease stress hormone production –

creating what he calls a "neural exercise" that strengthens our self-regulation capacity over time.

2. Cognitive Strategies: Changing Your Thinking

Once your physiological arousal has decreased enough to access your thinking brain, these cognitive strategies can help:

Thought Labeling: Simply naming your thoughts ("I'm having the thought that my partner doesn't respect me") creates distance and perspective.

Reality Testing: Ask yourself questions like "What evidence supports this interpretation? What evidence contradicts it? Are there other possible explanations?"

Perspective Broadening: Zoom out to see the bigger picture. "How important will this seem in a week? A month? A year?"

Values Reconnection: Remind yourself of what matters most to you in your relationship and how you want to show up as a partner.

Dr. Matthew Lieberman's neuroimaging research at UCLA has shown that the simple act of labeling emotions actually reduces activity in the amygdala while increasing activity in the prefrontal cortex – literally helping the thinking brain regain control from the emotional brain. His studies demonstrate that putting feelings into words (what he calls "affect labeling") is a powerful regulatory strategy accessible even during emotional distress.

3. Time-Out Protocol: When You Need Space

Sometimes the most responsible choice is to temporarily pause a difficult conversation until both partners can return to their windows of tolerance. However, taking a time-out needs to be done carefully to avoid it becoming another form of withdrawal or abandonment:

Establish the Protocol in Advance: During a calm moment, agree on how time-outs will work in your relationship.

Signal Respectfully: Use an agreed-upon phrase like "I need to take a regulation break" rather than storming off or shutting down.

Set a Specific Return Time: Always specify when you'll return to the conversation: "I need 20 minutes to calm down, and then I'll be ready to continue talking."

Use the Time Productively: During the break, actively use self-regulation strategies rather than ruminating or building your case.

Honor the Return Commitment: Always come back when you said you would, even if it's just to request more time. This builds trust that issues won't be permanently avoided.

Dr. John Gottman's research at the University of Washington has shown that taking structured breaks during conflict can be highly effective, but only when certain conditions are met. His studies found that couples who take productive time-outs show reduced physiological arousal (lower heart rates, decreased blood pressure) when they return to difficult conversations, while those who use breaks as avoidance strategies show no such improvement.

4. Mindfulness Practices: Building Your Regulation Muscles

Regular mindfulness practice strengthens your overall capacity for self-regulation, making it easier to stay within your window of tolerance even during challenging interactions:

Daily Meditation: Even 5-10 minutes of daily meditation has been shown to increase emotional regulation capacity.

Body Scanning: Regularly practice noticing physical sensations throughout your body without judgment, increasing your awareness of early signs of dysregulation.

Mindful Check-Ins: Set reminders to briefly check your emotional state throughout the day, building the habit of emotional awareness.

Self-Compassion Practice: Learn to respond to your own distress with kindness rather than self-criticism, which only increases stress and shame.

Dr. Richard Davidson's groundbreaking research at the University of Wisconsin-Madison has demonstrated that regular mindfulness practice actually changes brain structure and function in ways that enhance emotional regulation. Using advanced neuroimaging techniques, his team has documented increased gray matter density in brain regions associated with attention, sensory processing, and emotional regulation among long term meditation practitioners.

Similarly, Dr. Sara Lazar's research at Harvard Medical School has shown that even eight weeks of mindfulness practice produces measurable changes in brain regions associated

with emotional regulation, including increased cortical thickness in the prefrontal cortex and reduced volume in the amygdala.

Self-Regulation in Action: Practical Exercises

Exercise: The Emotional Fire Drill
Time needed: 30 minutes initial planning, then ongoing practice **Materials:** Paper and pen
Just as buildings have fire drills to prepare for emergencies, couples need "emotional fire drills" to prepare for moments of high emotional intensity:
- Together, identify a recurring challenging situation in your relationship (e.g., discussions

about finances, parenting disagreements, family visits).

- Individually, write down:

  ◦ Early warning signs that you're becoming triggered

  ◦ Specific self-regulation strategies that work for you

  ◦ What you need from your partner when you're becoming dysregulated

  ◦ How you'll signal if you need a time-out

Share your plans with each other and create a joint strategy for navigating these situations.
After the next real occurrence of this challenging situation, debrief together: What worked? What didn't? How can you refine your approach?

Exercise: The Trigger Journal

Time needed: 10 minutes per entry, as needed **Materials:** Journal or note-taking app After experiencing an emotional trigger in your relationship:

- Record what happened just before you felt triggered (the situation, words, behaviors).

- Note your physical sensations, thoughts, emotions, and behaviors in response.

- Reflect on any past experiences that might be connected to this trigger.

- Write down how you managed the trigger in the moment, what worked, and what you might try differently next time.

- Consider sharing relevant insights with your partner to increase mutual understanding.

Over time, this journal will reveal patterns and help you develop increasingly effective personalized regulation strategies.

Self-Regulation Across Different Relationship Phases

Self-regulation needs and strategies may vary depending on your relationship stage:

New Relationships

In the early phases of a relationship, strong emotions often stem from uncertainty, vulnerability, and the high stakes of new attachment. Self-regulation helps you:

- Manage anxiety about the relationship's future

- Avoid premature disclosure or emotional overwhelm

- Stay present rather than projecting past relationship patterns

- Make thoughtful choices rather than being driven solely by chemistry and excitement

Established Relationships

In long-term partnerships, self-regulation challenges often involve:

- Managing familiarity triggers (those buttons only your partner knows how to push)

- Avoiding complacency or emotional disengagement

- Navigating major life transitions together (career changes, parenthood, etc.)

- Preventing accumulated resentments from hijacking current interactions

Relationships in Crisis

During relationship challenges or conflicts, self-regulation becomes especially crucial for:

- Preventing permanent damage during temporary struggles

- Maintaining perspective during painful emotions

- Making decisions based on values rather than reactivity

- Creating space for healing and repair

Self-Regulation and Gender: Navigating Different Patterns

Research suggests that men and women sometimes differ in their emotional regulation patterns, though these are generalizations and don't apply to everyone:

Common patterns in male emotional regulation:

- May externalize emotions through action or problem-solving

- Often socialized to suppress vulnerable emotions like fear or sadness

- May experience emotions more physically than verbally

- Sometimes need physical space or activity to process emotions

Common patterns in female emotional regulation:

- May process emotions through verbal expression and connection

- Often socialized to suppress anger while expressing

vulnerability

- May experience emotions more relationally

- Sometimes need conversation and validation to process emotions

These differences aren't inherently problematic, but they can create misunderstandings when partners have different regulation needs and styles. The key is to understand and respect these differences rather than judging them.

For example, when a male partner withdraws during conflict, his female partner might interpret this as abandonment or lack of care, when he may actually be attempting to regulate his emotions to avoid saying something hurtful. Similarly, when a female partner wants to talk through an issue immediately, her male partner might interpret this as pressure or criticism, when she may be seeking connection as a way to regulate her distress.

Dialogue Scripts: Self-Regulation in Action

Here are some examples of language that facilitates self-regulation in different relationship contexts:

When you notice yourself becoming triggered: "I'm noticing I'm starting to feel defensive. I want to have this conversation, but I need a moment to collect my thoughts so I can respond thoughtfully rather than reactively."

When your partner seems triggered: "I can see this topic is bringing up strong feelings for you. Would it be helpful to take a short break, or would you prefer to continue but maybe slow down the conversation?"

When returning after a regulation break: "Thank you for giving me space to calm down. I'm feeling more centered now and ready to listen. I care about resolving this together."

When establishing regulation agreements: "I've noticed we both get overwhelmed during financial discussions. Could we create some agreements about how to handle those conversations in ways that help us both stay regulated?"

When acknowledging regulation patterns: "I've realized that when I feel criticized, I tend to shut down. That's not about you—it's my old pattern from childhood. I'm working on staying present even when those feelings come up."

Chapter Reflection: Your Self-Regulation Journey

Take a moment to reflect on self-regulation in your relationship:

1. What are your earliest memories of learning (or not learning) to regulate your emotions? How might these experiences influence your current patterns?

2. What situations or interactions with your partner most commonly trigger dysregulation for you? For them?

3. What self-regulation strategies have you found most effective? Which would you like to develop further?

4. How might improving your self-regulation skills change the dynamic in your relationship?

5. What's one small step you could take this week to expand your window of tolerance?

The Bridge to the Next Element: From Self-Regulation to Empathy

While self-regulation focuses on managing your own emotional responses, the next element of the P.U.L.S.E. framework—Empathy—extends this awareness outward to your partner's experience. In the next chapter, we'll explore how developing greater empathic understanding creates the foundation for deep connection, even across significant differences.

We'll discover how empathy builds on the skills of self-regulation, allowing you to remain present with your partner's emotions without becoming overwhelmed or defensive. You'll learn practical approaches to what relationship researchers call "emotional attunement"—the ability to sense, understand, and respond to your partner's emotional needs.

But before we move on, I encourage you to begin implementing at least one self regulation practice from this chapter. Remember that neural pathways strengthen through consistent activation—each effort to regulate your emotions literally reshapes your brain's regulatory circuits, gradually creating a relationship where both partners can navigate even intense emotions without damaging your connection.

LOVE WITH P.U.L.S.E.

KEEP GOING AFTER THE CHAPTER ENDS

- Guided Video Exercises
- Printable Worksheets
- Real-Life Tools You Can Use Today

Turn what you just read into what you can actually do — right now.

Dr. Ashley R. Bryant

Creator of the P.U.L.S.E. Framework & Author of Love With P.U.L.S.E.

Already finished the book? Scan to access every chapter's bonus content in one place.

Chapter 6
Empathize: The Heart of Connection

Empathy—the ability to understand and share the feelings of another—is perhaps the most transformative element of the P.U.L.S.E. framework. While understanding helps us comprehend our partner's perspective intellectually, and listening creates space for their expression, empathy is what allows us to truly connect with their emotional experience. It's the difference between knowing about someone's pain and feeling it alongside them; between acknowledging their joy and genuinely celebrating in it.

In this chapter, we'll explore the profound power of empathy in relationships, how it differs from sympathy or understanding, and most importantly, how to cultivate and express it even in challenging moments. We'll discover why empathy is not just a nice-to have quality but an essential foundation for lasting love and connection.

The Empathy Distinction: Beyond Understanding to Feeling

Empathy is often confused with sympathy or intellectual understanding, but it's distinctly different:

- **Understanding** is cognitive—grasping someone's perspective or situation intellectually.

- **Sympathy** is feeling for someone—recognizing their emotions and responding with compassion, but from a distance.

- **Empathy** is feeling with someone—temporarily stepping into their emotional experience as if it were your own.

This distinction is crucial. When your partner shares something difficult, understanding helps you make sense of it, sympathy prompts you to offer comfort, but empathy creates a profound connection where they feel truly seen and not alone in their experience.

The Neuroscience of Empathy

The human capacity for empathy has deep neurobiological roots. In the 1990s, neuroscientists led by Giacomo Rizzolatti at the University of Parma discovered "mirror neurons" in the brain that activate both when we perform an action and when we observe someone else performing that action. This revolutionary finding provided the first neural evidence for how we might understand others' experiences from the inside.

Subsequent research has revealed that empathy involves multiple brain networks working in concert:

1. **The Mirror Neuron System**: Located primarily in the premotor cortex and inferior parietal lobule, this system helps us understand others' actions and intentions by creating an internal simulation. When you see your partner wince in pain, your mirror neurons activate as if you were experiencing that pain yourself, creating the foundation for emotional resonance.

2. **The Limbic Resonance System**: This network, including the insula and anterior cingulate cortex, processes emotional contagion—our tendency to "catch" feelings from those around us. Dr. Daniel Siegel describes this as "feeling felt" by another person, a cornerstone of secure attachment.

3. **The Mentalizing Network**: Centered in the prefrontal cortex, temporoparietal junction, and posterior cingulate, this system helps us make inferences about others' mental states and differentiate their experience from our own. This allows for what researchers call "empathic accuracy"—correctly identifying what another person is thinking and feeling.

Dr. Helen Riess, a psychiatrist at Harvard Medical School, explains that these neural systems create what she calls the "empathy circuit"—a coordinated brain response that allows us to tune into others' emotional states. Her research shows that when this circuit functions optimally, partners experience a form of "neural synchrony" where their brain activity actually begins to mirror each other during moments of deep empathic connection.

What's particularly encouraging about this research is that these neural pathways can be strengthened through practice. Dr. Richard Davidson's work at the University of Wisconsin-Madison has shown that regular empathy exercises actually increase neural connectivity in these regions, making empathic responses more automatic and accurate over time.

Case Study: The Difference in Action

When Sophia lost a promotion she had been working toward for months, her partner Marcus had three possible responses:

Understanding response: "I see why you're upset. You put in so many extra hours and really deserved that promotion."

Sympathetic response: "I'm so sorry that happened. That's really unfair. Is there anything I can do to help?"

Empathetic response: Marcus sits beside Sophia, matches her body language, and says with genuine emotion, "This is crushing... all that work, all that hope... and then to have it not happen." His face reflects her disappointment, and he simply stays present with her in that difficult moment.

The understanding response acknowledged the facts. The sympathetic response offered comfort. But the empathetic response made Sophia feel truly seen and not alone in her disappointment. She later shared that it was Marcus's willingness to simply sit in the pain with her, without trying to fix it or move past it, that made her feel most loved.

The Science of Empathy: Mirror Neurons and Emotional Contagion

The human capacity for empathy has biological roots. Neuroscientists have discovered "mirror neurons" in our brains that activate both when we perform an action and when we observe someone else performing that action. This same mirroring system applies to emotions—when we see someone experiencing an emotion, our brains can activate as if we were experiencing it ourselves.

This explains the phenomenon of "emotional contagion"—how we can "catch" feelings from those around us. When your partner is genuinely happy, you may find yourself smiling without conscious effort. When they're anxious, you might start feeling tense yourself.

This biological capacity for emotional resonance is the foundation of empathy, and it serves a crucial evolutionary purpose: it helps us connect, cooperate, and care for each other. In intimate relationships, this empathic resonance creates the emotional glue that bonds partners together through shared experiences of joy, pain, fear, and hope.

Research shows that couples with higher levels of empathic responsiveness report greater relationship satisfaction, better conflict resolution, and deeper emotional intimacy. When partners feel empathically understood, they're more likely to be vulnerable, to trust, and to feel secure in the relationship.

The Three Dimensions of Empathy in Relationships

Relationship researcher Dr. John Gottman identifies three types of empathy that are particularly important in intimate relationships:

1. **Cognitive Empathy**: The ability to understand your partner's perspective and emotional state intellectually. This involves recognizing what they might be feeling and why.

2. **Emotional Empathy**: The capacity to actually feel something of what your partner is feeling—to resonate with their emotional experience.

3. **Compassionate Empathy**: Moving beyond understanding and feeling to taking supportive action based on your empathic connection.

All three dimensions are important in different contexts. Sometimes your partner primarily needs you to understand their perspective (cognitive empathy). Other times, they need to feel that you're emotionally present with them in their joy or pain (emotional empathy). And sometimes, they need you to translate that empathic understanding into supportive action (compassionate empathy).

Dr. Gottman's research at the University of Washington has shown that these different forms of empathy activate distinct neural circuits. Cognitive empathy primarily engages the prefrontal cortex and temporoparietal junction—regions associated with perspective-taking and theory of mind. Emotional empathy activates the insula and anterior cingulate cortex—areas involved in emotional processing and interoception (awareness of bodily sensations). Compassionate empathy additionally engages the periaqueductal gray and ventral striatum—regions linked to caregiving behavior and reward.

What's particularly interesting is that Gottman's longitudinal studies show that couples who demonstrate all three forms of empathy during conflict discussions are significantly more likely to remain together and report higher relationship satisfaction over time. His research found that the presence of empathic responses during disagreements was a stronger predictor of relationship longevity than the frequency or intensity of conflicts themselves.

Dialogue Example: The Three Dimensions in Action

Partner: "*I had the worst day at work. My presentation completely bombed, and I could see everyone was bored and checking their phones. I feel like such a failure.*"

Cognitive Empathy Response: "I can see why that would be really discouraging. You put so much work into that presentation, and having people not engage would feel like a rejection of your effort."

Emotional Empathy Response: (With matching facial expression and tone) "Oh no... that feeling of standing there watching people check out while you're speaking... that pit in your stomach... I can imagine how crushing that felt."

Compassionate Empathy Response: "That sounds really painful. I can feel how disappointed you are. Would it help to talk through what happened, or would you prefer some quiet time together to decompress first? I'm here either way."

Barriers to Empathy: What Gets in Our Way

Despite our innate capacity for empathy, several factors can block or diminish our ability to empathize effectively with our partners:

- **Self-Preoccupation**: When we're overwhelmed with our own concerns, stresses, or emotions, we have less bandwidth available for empathic connection.

- **Defensive Posture**: When we feel criticized or attacked, our self-protective instincts can override our empathic capabilities.

- **Empathy Fatigue**: Continuous empathic engagement without self-care can lead to emotional depletion and reduced capacity for empathy.

- **Assumption of Similarity**: Believing our partner's experience must be similar to how we would feel in their situation can lead to misguided responses.

- **Fear of Emotional Contagion**: Sometimes we resist empathy because we're afraid of being pulled into difficult emotions ourselves.

- **Judgment and Criticism**: When we're judging our partner's feelings or reactions as inappropriate or irrational, we block our ability to connect empathically.

- **Solution Focus**: Rushing to solve problems rather than first connecting emotionally can bypass the empathic moment your partner needs.

From a neurobiological perspective, these barriers make perfect sense. When we feel threatened or overwhelmed, the brain's executive function networks – regions responsible for empathy, perspective-taking, and emotional regulation – become less active. Dr. Daniel Siegel calls this process "flipping our lid" – when our higher cognitive functions become temporarily unavailable due to emotional arousal.

Dr. Brené Brown's research on empathy and vulnerability helps explain why empathy can sometimes feel risky. Her studies show that truly empathizing with another person requires us to access our own experiences of similar emotions—what she calls "emotional courage." When we're afraid of our own vulnerability, we may unconsciously block empathic connection as a form of self-protection.

Understanding these neurobiological and psychological barriers helps explain why empathy can be challenging even in loving relationships. It's not just a matter of willpower or intention – our brains are literally designed to prioritize self-protection over connection when we feel threatened or overwhelmed.

Exercise : The Emotion Journal Exchange
Time needed: 15 minutes writing, 20 minutes sharing
Materials: Journals or paper, pens
1. Separately, each partner writes about a significant emotional experience from their past (not related to the current relationship). Describe not just what happened, but the full emotional landscape—how it felt physically, what thoughts accompanied the feelings, how the emotions shifted over time.
2. Take turns reading your entries to each other. The listening partner focuses on imagining themselves in the described experience, trying to feel some of what their partner felt.
3. After each reading, the listener shares what emotions they connected with and asks questions to deepen their understanding of their partner's experience.

This exercise builds empathic capacity by practicing emotional connection with experiences outside your current relationship dynamics, making it safer to explore vulnerable feelings.

Exercise: The Daily Empathy Check-In
Time needed: 5-10 minutes daily **Materials:** None
Establish a daily ritual of brief empathic connection:

- At a consistent time each day (perhaps before dinner or before bed), take turns sharing the emotional high point and low point of your day.

- The listening partner practices empathic responses, focusing on connecting with the emotion rather than discussing the details or offering solutions.

- Keep the exchange brief—just a few minutes each—but make it a priority to truly connect with each other's emotional experience.

This simple daily practice builds the habit of empathic connection and ensures that partners regularly update their understanding of each other's emotional worlds.

Empathy During Conflict: The Ultimate Relationship Skill

Perhaps the most challenging—and most transformative—application of empathy is during relationship conflict. When we're hurt, angry, or feeling misunderstood, our natural tendency is to focus on our own experience and perspective. Yet this is precisely when empathy can have its most powerful impact.

Research by Dr. John Gottman shows that successful conflict resolution depends not on finding the perfect solution, but on how partners connect emotionally during the disagreement. Couples who can maintain empathic connection even while discussing difficult topics are significantly more likely to find mutually satisfying resolutions and to feel closer after conflicts.

Dr. Gottman's groundbreaking "Love Lab" research identified specific physiological markers of empathic connection during conflict. Using measures like heart rate, blood pressure, and stress hormone levels, his team found that partners who maintained empathic engagement during disagreements showed dramatically different physiological patterns than those who became emotionally disconnected.

Specifically, empathically connected partners demonstrated what Gottman calls "physiological soothing"—the ability to help regulate each other's stress response even during disagreement. Their heart rates remained lower, their stress hormones didn't spike as dramatically, and they recovered more quickly after difficult discussions.

This physiological data provides compelling evidence for why empathy matters so much during conflict. It's not just about feeling understood—empathic connection literally helps regulate our nervous systems during stress, allowing us to stay present and engaged rather than becoming overwhelmed or shutting down.

The Empathic Conflict Process

Here's a structured approach to maintaining empathy during disagreements:

1. **Begin with Self-Regulation**: Use the skills from the previous chapter to ensure you're in your window of tolerance before attempting empathic connection.

2. **Lead with Curiosity, Not Certainty**: Approach your partner's perspective with genuine curiosity rather than assuming you already understand their position.

3. **Validate Before Problem-Solving**: Ensure your partner feels emotionally understood before moving to solutions. "I can see why you'd feel that way" doesn't mean you agree, just that you recognize their feelings make sense from their perspective.

4. **Look for the Underlying Need**: Often conflicts arise from unmet needs that aren't initially obvious. Practice asking, "What's important to you about this?" to uncover deeper concerns.

5. **Find the Common Ground**: Even in disagreement, there are usually shared values or goals. Identifying these creates a foundation for collaborative problem-solving.

Case Study: Empathy Transforming Conflict

Elena and Carlos had been arguing about finances for months. Elena wanted to save aggressively for a house down payment, while Carlos felt they should enjoy more experiences now while they were young and healthy.

Their typical pattern was to debate the practical merits of each approach, with Elena citing financial experts about the benefits of homeownership and Carlos countering with research on how experiences create more lasting happiness than possessions. These conversations inevitably ended in frustration and distance.

In therapy, they learned to approach the conflict with empathy first. When they next discussed the topic, instead of immediately advocating for their positions, they each tried to understand the emotional drivers behind their partner's perspective.

Elena discovered that Carlos's desire for experiences was rooted in watching his father work tirelessly to pay for a house, only to develop a serious illness shortly after achieving that goal. His father never got to enjoy the travel dreams he had deferred.

Carlos learned that Elena's focus on homeownership stemmed from childhood housing insecurity after her parents' divorce forced frequent moves between increasingly affordable apartments. A home represented stability and security she had never known growing up.

With this empathic understanding, they were able to develop a financial plan that addressed both needs—allocating funds for meaningful experiences now while still making progress toward the security of homeownership. More importantly, they felt genuinely understood by each other, transforming a source of conflict into an opportunity for deeper connection.

Limbic Resonance and Relationship Bonding

Psychiatrists Thomas Lewis, Fari Amini, and Richard Lannon introduced the concept of "limbic resonance" in their influential book "A General Theory of Love." They describe it as "a symphony of mutual exchange and internal adaptation whereby two mammals become attuned to each other's inner states."

This resonance occurs at a neurobiological level through what scientists call "interbrain neural coupling" – a phenomenon where the brain activity of two people in close relationship begins to synchronize. Dr. Uri Hasson's research at Princeton University has demonstrated this synchronization using functional MRI, showing that during deep empathic connection, partners' neural patterns actually begin to mirror each other.

This limbic resonance creates what attachment researchers call a "secure base" – the feeling of emotional safety that allows us to be vulnerable, take risks, and grow within relationships. Dr. Sue Johnson explains that this secure base is established and maintained primarily through empathic responsiveness – the consistent experience of being emotionally seen, understood, and valued by our partner.

What's particularly fascinating about limbic resonance is that it operates largely outside conscious awareness. Our nervous systems are constantly reading and responding to our partner's emotional cues through what neuroscientists call "implicit processing" – the rapid, automatic assessment of emotional information that happens before conscious thought. This explains why we can often sense our partner's emotional state before they've said a word, and why empathic connection feels so immediate and powerful.

Self-Empathy: The Foundation for Partner Empathy

An often overlooked aspect of relationship empathy is self-empathy—the ability to connect with, understand, and validate your own emotional experience. Without this foundation, attempts to empathize with your partner may be limited or unsustainable.

Self-empathy involves:

- Recognizing and naming your own emotions without judgment

- Understanding the valid needs and values underlying your feelings

- Treating yourself with the same compassion you would offer a loved one

- Allowing yourself to feel difficult emotions rather than suppressing or avoiding them

When you practice self-empathy, you expand your emotional vocabulary and awareness, which directly enhances your ability to empathize with others. You also become less reactive when triggered, as you can hold space for your own emotions without immediately acting on them.

Dr. Kristin Neff's research on self-compassion provides scientific support for the importance of self-empathy. Her studies show that people with higher levels of self compassion demonstrate greater emotional resilience, less anxiety and depression, and more satisfying relationships. Importantly, her research contradicts the common fear that self-compassion leads to self-indulgence or lowered standards – in fact, people with higher self-compassion actually take more responsibility for their actions and show greater motivation for personal growth.

From a neurobiological perspective, self-empathy activates the caregiving system in the brain – the same regions involved in compassion toward others. Dr. Richard Davidson's research shows that practices like mindful self-compassion increase activity in the prefrontal cortex while decreasing activity in the amygdala, creating a brain state more conducive to empathic connection with others.

Exercise: Cultivating Self-Empathy

Time needed: 10-15 minutes **Materials:** Journal or paper, pen

Think of a recent situation where you experienced difficult emotions.

- Write about the situation briefly, then focus on your emotional experience:

  - What emotions were present? (Try to be specific beyond basic labels like "bad" or "upset")

  - Where did you feel these emotions in your body?

  - What thoughts accompanied these feelings?

  - What needs or values of yours were involved?

- Write a brief self-empathic response, as if you were responding to a dear friend with the same experience. Use language of validation and compassion.

- Notice how this self-empathic stance affects your

relationship to the difficult emotions.

- Regular practice of this exercise builds the foundation for greater empathic capacity with your partner.

Empathy Across Difference: Bridging Emotional Worlds

Some of the most powerful opportunities for empathic connection occur across significant differences in emotional experience or expression. Partners often have different emotional languages, sensitivities, and patterns—differences that can create disconnection if approached with judgment, but that can become sources of growth and enrichment when approached with empathy.

Common Empathy Gaps in Relationships

- **Different emotional intensities**: One partner experiences emotions more intensely than the other.

- **Different emotional vocabularies**: Partners have varying abilities to identify and articulate emotional states.

- **Different comfort with vulnerability**: Partners may have different thresholds for emotional disclosure.

- **Different emotional triggers**: What deeply affects one partner may barely register for the other.

- **Different emotional regulation styles**: Partners may have contrasting approaches to managing difficult feelings.

Bridging the Gaps with Empathic Curiosity

The key to bridging these differences is what psychologists call "empathic curiosity"—a genuine interest in your partner's unique emotional world without judgment or assumption. This curiosity transforms differences from sources of frustration to opportunities for deeper understanding.

Questions that foster empathic curiosity include:

- "What is this feeling like for you?"
- "How do you experience anger/sadness/fear in your body?"
- "What helps you feel safe when you're upset?"
- "What did you learn about this emotion growing up?"
- "What do you need when you feel this way?"

Dialogue Scripts: Empathy in Action

Here are some examples of language that facilitates empathic connection in different relationship contexts:

When your partner shares a difficult experience: "That sounds really painful. I'm trying to imagine what that felt like for you... was it something like feeling exposed and judged? Or was it different from that?"

When you notice your partner seems upset: "I'm noticing you seem upset right now. I'd like to understand what you're feeling, if you want to share it."

When empathizing across difference: "I know I might not react the same way in that situation, but I want to understand how it felt for you. Can you help me see it through your eyes?"

When empathizing during conflict: "Even though we see this differently, I really want to understand your perspective. What feels most important to you about this?"

When offering empathy for joy: "I can see how excited you are about this! Tell me more about what makes this so meaningful for you—I want to celebrate this with you."

Chapter Reflection: Your Empathy Patterns

Take a moment to reflect on empathy in your relationship:

1. In what situations do you find it easiest to empathize with your partner? Most difficult?

2. How was empathy modeled (or not modeled) in your family of origin? How might this influence your current empathic patterns?

3. Which dimension of empathy (cognitive, emotional, or compassionate) comes most naturally to you? Which is most challenging?

4. What are your personal barriers to empathy? What gets in the way of your empathic connection?

5. How might developing greater empathy—both for yourself and your partner— transform your relationship?

The Bridge to Integration: Bringing the P.U.L.S.E. Elements Together

We've now explored all five elements of the P.U.L.S.E. framework: Praise, Understand, Listen, Self-regulate, and Empathize. While we've examined each element separately for clarity, in practice, they work together as an integrated system, each supporting and enhancing the others.

In the next chapter, we'll explore how to integrate these elements into a cohesive approach to relationship enhancement. We'll discover how conflicts can actually become opportunities for deeper connection when approached with the P.U.L.S.E. framework, and how to create a relationship environment where love and understanding can flourish even through life's challenges.

But before we move on, I encourage you to begin implementing at least one empathy practice from this chapter. Remember that neural pathways strengthen through consistent activation—each effort to connect empathically literally reshapes your brain's empathy circuits, gradually creating a relationship where both partners feel deeply seen, understood, and valued in their unique emotional experience.

LOVE WITH P.U.L.S.E.

KEEP GOING AFTER THE CHAPTER ENDS

- Guided Video Exercises
- Printable Worksheets
- Real-Life Tools You Can Use Today

Turn what you just read into what you can actually do — right now.

Dr. Ashley R. Bryant

Creator of the P.U.L.S.E. Framework & Author of Love With P.U.L.S.E.

Already finished the book? Scan to access every chapter's bonus content in one place.

CHAPTER 7
Conflict as Connection

Conflict. The very word can trigger tension in our bodies and anxiety in our minds. In our culture, conflict is often viewed as something to be avoided at all costs—a sign that something is wrong with a relationship, a failure of communication, or evidence of incompatibility. But what if I told you that conflict, when approached skillfully, could actually be one of the most powerful opportunities for deepening connection and intimacy in your relationship?

In this chapter, we'll explore how the P.U.L.S.E. framework—Praise, Understanding, Listening, Self-regulation, and Empathy—comes together to transform conflict from a threat to your relationship into a catalyst for growth and deeper connection. We'll discover why conflict is not only inevitable but necessary in healthy relationships, and how to navigate disagreements in ways that strengthen rather than damage your bond.

The Paradox of Conflict in Intimate Relationships

Here's a truth that might surprise you: the complete absence of conflict in a relationship is not a sign of health—it's often a warning sign. Couples who report never arguing are frequently engaging in conflict avoidance, which can lead to emotional distance, unresolved issues, and simmering resentment.

Healthy relationships aren't characterized by an absence of conflict but by how conflicts are approached and resolved. When handled with skill and care, disagreements can actually bring partners closer together, deepen understanding, and strengthen trust. This is the paradox of conflict in intimate relationships—what seems like a threat to connection can become its catalyst.

Case Study: The Avoidance Trap

Michael and Jen prided themselves on their "perfect" relationship. They rarely argued and considered this a sign of their compatibility. But beneath the surface, tensions were building. Michael felt Jen spent too much time at work but never brought it up, not wanting to seem unsupportive of her career. Jen was increasingly frustrated by Michael's messiness but kept quiet to avoid seeming nagging or critical.

Over time, these unaddressed issues created emotional distance. Michael started spending more evenings out with friends, while Jen threw herself even more into work. When they finally sought therapy, they realized their avoidance of conflict had prevented them from truly knowing each other's needs and concerns. Their "perfect" relationship had become a polite partnership between two increasingly disconnected people.

Through therapy, they learned to view conflict as an opportunity for growth rather than a threat. As they began to express their true feelings and needs—even when it created temporary tension—they paradoxically felt closer and more connected than they had in years.

The Science of Conflict: What Research Reveals

Dr. John Gottman's groundbreaking research with thousands of couples has revealed fascinating insights about conflict in relationships:

1. **All couples have perpetual problems**: About 69% of relationship conflicts are about recurring issues that will never be fully resolved because they stem from fundamental differences in personality, values, or needs. The key to relationship success isn't solving these unsolvable problems but learning to dialogue about them constructively.

2. **It's not about whether you fight, but how you fight**: Couples who stay happily together for the long term aren't those who avoid conflict—they're those who manage conflict in ways that maintain respect and connection.

3. **The first three minutes predict the outcome**: How a conflict discussion begins is crucial. If it starts with harsh criticism, contempt, or defensiveness, it's likely to end negatively regardless of attempts to repair later.

4. **Emotional flooding derails resolution**: When partners become physiologically flooded with stress hormones

during conflict, their ability to think clearly, listen empathically, and problem-solve effectively is severely compromised.

5. **Successful repair attempts are crucial**: All couples make mistakes during conflict. What distinguishes happy couples is their ability to make and receive repair attempts—efforts to de-escalate tension and reconnect.

The P.U.L.S.E. Approach to Conflict

The five elements of the P.U.L.S.E. framework provide a comprehensive approach to transforming how you experience and navigate conflict in your relationship:

P - Praise: Maintaining a culture of appreciation creates a positive emotional bank account that buffers against the negativity of conflicts. During disagreements, finding something to genuinely appreciate about your partner's perspective can de-escalate tension.

U - Understanding: Seeking to understand your partner's perspective before advocating for your own creates space for collaborative rather than adversarial problem-solving.

L - Listening: Deep, empathic listening during conflict allows you to hear not just your partner's position but the needs, values, and feelings underlying it.

S - Self-regulation: Managing your own emotional reactions prevents the escalation that occurs when both partners become flooded and reactive.

E - Empathy: Connecting with your partner's emotional experience, even when you disagree with their perspective, maintains the emotional bond that makes resolution possible.

Dialogue Example: The P.U.L.S.E. Approach in Action

Partner A: "I'm really frustrated that you made plans for us this weekend without checking with me first. I had been looking forward to some quiet time at home."

Partner B (without P.U.L.S.E.): "You're always complaining about our social life being boring, and now you're mad that I made plans? I can't win with you!"

Partner B (with P.U.L.S.E.):

Praise: "I appreciate that you're being direct about how you're feeling instead of just silently being upset."

Understanding: "Let me make sure I understand—you were looking forward to downtime at home this weekend, and my making plans without consulting you felt like your needs weren't considered?"

Listening: "Tell me more about what you were hoping for this weekend. What kind of rest or activities were you looking forward to?"

Self-regulation: (notices rising defensiveness and takes a deep breath before responding calmly)

Empathy: "I can see how that would be disappointing when you've been looking forward to relaxing at home. That makes perfect sense, especially after the busy week you've had."

"I didn't realize you were counting on downtime this weekend. I was excited about these plans and wanted to surprise you, but I see now that checking with you first would have been better. Maybe we can find a compromise that gives you some of the rest you need while still keeping some of these plans?"

Common Conflict Patterns and How to Transform Them

Most couples fall into predictable patterns during conflict. Recognizing your pattern is the first step toward changing it. Here are some of the most common:

1. The Pursuer-Distancer Dynamic

In this pattern, one partner pursues or criticizes while the other distances or withdraws. The more one pursues, the more the other withdraws, creating a self-reinforcing cycle that leaves both partners frustrated.

Transformation Strategy:

- The pursuing partner practices softening their approach, leading with "I" statements about feelings rather than criticisms

- The distancing partner commits to staying engaged, even if just to say, "I'm feeling overwhelmed and need a short break, but I promise to return to this conversation at [specific time]"

- Both partners recognize their roles in the pattern and work together to create a new dynamic

2. The Criticism-Defensiveness Cycle

One partner criticizes, the other becomes defensive, which leads to more criticism, more defensiveness, and escalation.

Transformation Strategy:

- Replace criticism with specific requests: "Could you please text when you'll be late?" instead of "You're always late and inconsiderate!"

- Replace defensiveness with responsibility-taking: "You're right that I didn't text, and I can see how that affected you" instead of "Well, you're late all the time too!"

- Practice the pause: When you feel criticized or defensive, pause before responding to choose a more constructive response

3. The Flooding-Stonewalling Pattern

When emotional intensity becomes overwhelming, one or both partners may experience flooding—a physiological state where heart rate increases, stress hormones surge, and the ability to communicate effectively plummets. This often leads to stonewalling— emotionally shutting down or physically leaving the conversation.

Transformation Strategy:

- Recognize the physical signs of flooding early (racing heart, shallow breathing, feeling "zoned out")

- Implement a pre-agreed time-out protocol: "I'm feeling flooded and need 20 minutes to calm down. Let's continue this at 3:30."

- Use self-regulation techniques during the break (deep breathing, progressive muscle relaxation)

- Honor the commitment to return to the conversation once regulated

4. The Contempt Trap

Contempt—communicating from a position of superiority through sarcasm, eye-rolling, mockery, or hostile humor—is the most destructive pattern in relationships and the strongest predictor of divorce.

Transformation Strategy:

- Build a culture of appreciation to counteract contempt

- Practice expressing specific complaints rather than global criticisms

- When you notice contempt arising, pause and reconnect with what you value about your partner

- If contempt has become habitual, consider professional help, as this pattern can be particularly difficult to change without support

Practical Exercises: Transforming Your Conflict Patterns

Exercise: The Repair Inventory

Time needed: 30-45 minutes **Materials:** Paper and pens
This exercise helps couples develop personalized repair strategies:
Separately, each partner writes answers to these questions:

- What are 3-5 things your partner could say or do during a conflict that would help you feel more connected?

- What are 3-5 repair attempts you've made in the past that seemed effective?

- What are 3-5 repair attempts your partner has made that worked well for you?

Share your lists with each other and discuss patterns or themes.

Together, create a "Repair Menu"—a list of specific phrases, gestures, or actions that either of you can use during conflict to de-escalate tension and reconnect. Place this menu somewhere visible or accessible for reference during future disagreements.

Examples might include:

- "Can we start over?"

- "I care more about us than being right."

- A specific inside joke that breaks tension

- A 20-second hug

- "I'm feeling flooded. Can we take a 20-minute break and come back to this?"

The Art of the Complaint: How to Raise Issues Effectively

How you start a difficult conversation is crucial—research shows that the first three minutes of a conflict discussion predict with 96% accuracy how that conflict will end. Here's a structured approach to raising concerns in a way that minimizes defensiveness and maximizes the chance of productive dialogue:

The Gentle Startup Formula

1. **Begin with "I" not "You"**: Start with your feelings and experience rather than accusations about your partner's behavior.

2. **Describe the situation objectively**: Stick to observable facts without interpretation or judgment.

3. **Express your feelings**: Name your emotional response clearly and specifically.

4. **Connect to a need or value**: Explain why this matters to you—what need or value is at stake.

5. **Make a positive, specific request**: Ask for what you do want rather than complaining about what you don't want.

Example:

Instead of: "You never help around the house. You're so lazy and inconsiderate!"

Try: "I've noticed the dishes have been piling up this week (observation). I'm feeling overwhelmed and a bit resentful (feeling) because I value shared responsibility in our home (need/value). Would you be willing to take care of the kitchen cleanup after dinner tonight while I handle the laundry (specific request)?"

When Values Clash: Navigating Your Deepest Differences

Some of the most challenging conflicts arise when core values differ. These might include differences in:

- Financial priorities (saving vs. spending)
- Parenting approaches (permissive vs. structured)
- Social preferences (introverted vs. extroverted needs)
- Religious or political beliefs
- Family boundaries (involvement with extended family)

These value-based conflicts often feel particularly threatening because they touch on our identity and deeply held beliefs about what's right or important.

Case Study: Bridging a Values Gap

Elena and Marcus struggled with different approaches to money. Elena, who grew up in financial insecurity, valued saving and financial prudence above all. Marcus, raised in a family that used money to create experiences and memories, valued spontaneity and enjoyment of resources in the present.

Their initial attempts to discuss finances always ended in frustration, with Elena feeling anxious and Marcus feeling controlled. Through couples therapy, they learned to approach this values difference differently:

First, they each explored the origins of their money values—how their family histories and experiences shaped their perspectives.

Next, they identified the positive intentions behind each other's approach: Elena's desire for security and Marcus's desire for joy and memorable experiences.

Finally, they created a financial plan that honored both values: automatic savings that gave Elena peace of mind, combined with a dedicated "experience fund" that allowed Marcus to plan special activities without guilt or conflict.

The key wasn't that either person changed their core values, but that they found ways to honor both sets of values in their shared financial life.

When to Seek Help: Recognizing the Need for Support

While many conflicts can be navigated successfully using the principles and practices in this book, some situations benefit from professional support:

- When the same conflicts recur with increasing intensity and no resolution
- When one or both partners feel unsafe during disagreements
- When contempt has become a regular feature of your interactions
- When past traumas are being triggered by current conflicts
- When external stressors (job loss, illness, grief) overwhelm your coping resources
- When infidelity or trust violations have occurred

Seeking help isn't a sign of failure—it's a sign of commitment to your relationship's health and longevity. A skilled couples therapist can provide tools, perspective, and a safe space to work through challenging issues.

Dialogue Scripts: Navigating Common Conflict Scenarios

Here are examples of how to apply the P.U.L.S.E. approach to common relationship conflicts:

When discussing division of household labor: "I've been feeling overwhelmed lately with managing the household tasks (feeling). I notice I've been doing most of the cleaning and organizing (observation). I value partnership and shared responsibility in our home (value). Could we take some time this weekend to create a more balanced plan for household management that works for both of us (request)?"

When navigating different social needs: "I appreciate that you enjoy socializing and connecting with friends (praise). I understand these gatherings energize you and are important for your wellbeing (understanding). I've noticed I've been feeling drained after our busy social calendar lately (observation). Would you be open to finding a balance that allows for both social time and some quieter weekends at home (request)?"

When discussing financial decisions: "I know you're excited about this purchase and I can see why it appeals to you (empathy). I'm feeling anxious about the timing because of our upcoming expenses (feeling). Could we look at our budget together and see if there's a way to plan for this that feels comfortable for both of us (request)?"

Chapter Reflection: Your Conflict Patterns

Take a moment to reflect on your current conflict patterns in your relationship:

    1. What are your most recurring conflicts? Are they

about situational issues or deeper values differences?

2. How do you typically approach conflict—do you tend to pursue, distance, criticize, defend, or something else?

3. What are your early warning signs that you're becoming emotionally flooded during conflict?

4. What repair attempts have been effective in your relationship?

5. What's one specific way you could improve how you navigate conflict with your partner?

The Bridge to the Next Chapter: From Conflict to Intimacy

Successfully navigating conflict creates a foundation for deeper intimacy—the subject of our next chapter. When partners can disagree while maintaining respect and connection, they develop greater trust in the relationship's ability to withstand challenges. This security, in turn, allows for greater vulnerability and openness in all aspects of the relationship.

In the next chapter, we'll explore how to build intimacy beyond romance—creating deep connection across emotional, intellectual, spiritual, and physical dimensions. You'll discover how the P.U.L.S.E. framework can enhance all these aspects of intimacy, creating a relationship that is not just conflict-resilient but deeply fulfilling and life enriching.

But before we move on, I encourage you to begin practicing the conflict transformation exercises in this chapter. Remember that changing conflict patterns takes time and patience. Each difficult conversation you navigate with greater skill builds your capacity for the next one, gradually transforming conflict from a threat to your relationship into an opportunity for deeper understanding and connection.

LOVE WITH P.U.L.S.E.

KEEP GOING AFTER THE CHAPTER ENDS

- Guided Video Exercises
- Printable Worksheets
- Real-Life Tools You Can Use Today

Turn what you just read into what you can actually do — right now.

Dr. Ashley R. Bryant

Creator of the P.U.L.S.E. Framework & Author of Love With P.U.L.S.E.

Already finished the book? Scan to access every chapter's bonus content in one place.

Chapter 8
Building Intimacy Beyond Romance

When we think of intimacy in relationships, our minds often jump immediately to physical or romantic connection. While that aspect is certainly important, true intimacy encompasses so much more. In its fullest expression, intimacy is a multi-dimensional connection that touches every aspect of our shared lives—emotional, intellectual, spiritual, experiential, and yes, physical too.

In this chapter, we'll explore how to build and nurture these various dimensions of intimacy, creating a relationship that's not just romantically passionate but deeply connected across all levels of human experience. We'll see how the P.U.L.S.E. framework —Praise, Understanding, Listening, Self-regulation, and Empathy—provides the foundation for this rich, multifaceted intimacy.

The Five Dimensions of Intimacy

Truly fulfilling relationships cultivate connection across five key dimensions:

1. **Emotional Intimacy**: The ability to share your

authentic feelings, vulnerabilities, dreams, and fears with your partner, and to receive theirs with acceptance and care.

2. **Intellectual Intimacy**: Connecting through the exchange of ideas, thoughts, and perspectives; engaging each other's minds and respecting each other's viewpoints even when they differ.

3. **Experiential Intimacy**: Creating shared experiences and memories; having adventures together and developing rituals that are meaningful to both of you.

4. **Spiritual Intimacy**: Connecting around life's deeper questions—meaning, purpose, values, and beliefs—regardless of whether you share the same formal religious or spiritual tradition.

5. **Physical Intimacy**: Sharing physical closeness, from casual touch and affection to sexual connection, in ways that feel fulfilling and affirming to both partners.

These dimensions are interconnected and mutually reinforcing. Growth in one area often naturally enhances others. For example, deeper emotional intimacy frequently leads to more fulfilling physical intimacy, while shared experiences can foster greater intellectual and spiritual connection.

Case Study: The Intimacy Imbalance

David and Sophia had been married for eight years when they sought therapy. From the outside, their relationship looked ideal—they rarely argued, maintained an active social life, and were financially stable. But privately, both felt a growing sense of disconnection.

Through therapy, they realized they had developed a lopsided intimacy profile. They excelled at experiential intimacy (traveling together, socializing with friends) and maintained a reasonably satisfying physical relationship. However, they had neglected emotional intimacy—rarely sharing their deeper feelings, fears, or vulnerabilities—and had fallen into a pattern of avoiding meaningful conversations about their individual beliefs and values (spiritual intimacy).

This imbalance left them feeling like "friendly roommates" rather than deeply connected partners. They knew the surface details of each other's lives but had lost touch with each other's inner worlds.

Their journey back to connection involved deliberately cultivating the dimensions of intimacy they had neglected, particularly creating space for vulnerable emotional sharing and conversations about life's bigger questions. As these dimensions strengthened, they found their physical intimacy and shared experiences also became more meaningful and connecting.

Emotional Intimacy: The Courage to Be Seen

Emotional intimacy—the ability to share your authentic self and to truly see your partner —forms the foundation for all other types of connection. It requires vulnerability, trust, and the willingness to risk being truly known.

Many couples struggle with emotional intimacy because it requires facing our own insecurities and fears of rejection. We might worry: "If they really knew this about me, would they still love me?" This fear can lead to emotional withholding, where we share only the parts of ourselves that feel safe or acceptable.

The P.U.L.S.E. Approach to Emotional Intimacy

Praise: Acknowledging and appreciating your partner's emotional sharing creates safety for continued vulnerability. "Thank you for trusting me with that. It means so much that you feel safe sharing your fears with me."

Understanding: Making the effort to truly comprehend your partner's emotional landscape, including the history and experiences that shaped it.

Listening: Giving your full attention when your partner shares emotionally significant thoughts or feelings, without interrupting or immediately trying to fix their emotions.

Self-regulation: Managing your own reactions when your partner shares something that triggers you, so you can remain present and supportive.

Empathy: Connecting with your partner's emotional experience, even when it differs from how you might feel in a similar situation.

> **Exercise: Emotional Intimacy Building**
> **Time needed:** 30 minutes, once or twice weekly
> **Materials:** A comfortable, private space; optional journal
> This exercise, adapted from psychologist Arthur Aron's research on fostering closeness, helps build emotional intimacy through progressively deeper sharing:
> - Set aside uninterrupted time in a comfortable setting.
> - Take turns answering one question from each category below, with the listener practicing active listening without interruption:
>   - **Level 1 (Moderately Personal):**
>   - "What's something you've been proud of recently that you haven't shared with many people?
>   - "What's a fear or insecurity that sometimes affects your daily life?"
>   - "When was the last time you felt truly

vulnerable, and what was that experience like?"

- **Level 2 (More Personal):**

  - "What's something you've never told me about your childhood that shaped who you are?"

  - "What's a dream or aspiration you have that you rarely talk about?"

  - "When do you feel most emotionally disconnected from me, and what happens inside you during those times?"

- **Level 3 (Deeply Personal):**

  - "What's your greatest fear about our relationship?"

  - "When have you felt most emotionally exposed or hurt in our relationship, and what helped you move through that?"

  - "What do you need from me emotionally that's hard for you to ask for?"

- After each person shares, the listener reflects back what they heard and asks one thoughtful follow-up question before switching roles.

- End the exercise by expressing appreciation for what you learned about each other.

Intellectual Intimacy: Meeting of the Minds

Intellectual intimacy involves engaging with each other's thoughts, ideas, and perspectives in ways that stimulate and respect both minds. It's about connecting through curiosity, learning, and the exchange of viewpoints—even when those viewpoints differ.

Many couples underestimate the importance of intellectual connection, but research shows that mental stimulation and the ability to engage in meaningful conversation are significant factors in long-term relationship satisfaction.

The P.U.L.S.E. Approach to Intellectual Intimacy

Praise: Expressing genuine appreciation for your partner's thoughts and insights, even (especially) when they differ from your own. "I love how you think about these issues—you always bring perspectives I wouldn't have considered."

Understanding: Making the effort to grasp your partner's intellectual framework—how they process information and form opinions.

Listening: Engaging with your partner's ideas with genuine curiosity rather than waiting for your turn to speak or planning your rebuttal.

Self-regulation: Managing defensive reactions when your partner expresses ideas that challenge your own views.

Empathy: Connecting with the values and experiences that inform your partner's intellectual positions, even when you disagree with their conclusions.

> **Exercise: Intellectual Connection Building**
> **Time needed:** 45-60 minutes, monthly or as desired
> **Materials:** Books, articles, podcasts, or documentaries of mutual interest
> This exercise helps cultivate intellectual intimacy through shared exploration of ideas:
> Together, select something thought-provoking to both experience—a book, article, podcast episode, documentary, or lecture on a topic of mutual interest. Experience it separately first, making notes about your thoughts, questions, and reactions. Schedule a "discussion date" where you share your perspectives, using these prompts:
> - What was your strongest reaction or response?
> - What's one idea that challenged your thinking?
> - How does this connect to your own values or experiences?
> - What questions did it raise for you?
>
> Practice intellectual curiosity by asking follow-up questions about each other's perspectives rather than

simply stating your own views. End by identifying one new insight you gained from your partner's perspective.

Experiential Intimacy: Creating a Shared Story

Experiential intimacy develops through shared activities, adventures, challenges, and rituals that create a common history and sense of "us." These shared experiences become the stories you tell, the inside jokes you share, and the foundation of your unique couple identity.

Research shows that couples who regularly engage in novel experiences together report higher relationship satisfaction and passion over time. These shared adventures— whether grand or modest—create neurochemical responses similar to those experienced in early romantic love, helping to maintain excitement and connection in long-term relationships.

The P.U.L.S.E. Approach to Experiential Intimacy

Praise: Expressing appreciation for the unique qualities your partner brings to shared experiences. "I love how your spontaneity led us to discover that amazing hidden beach!"

Understanding: Recognizing that you may have different preferences for types of experiences and finding activities that honor both sets of needs.

Listening: Being attentive to your partner's experience during shared activities, noticing what brings them joy or discomfort.

Self-regulation: Managing your reactions when shared experiences don't go as planned or when your preferences differ.

Empathy: Connecting with your partner's experience of an activity, even when it differs from your own.

Exercise: Experience Building

Time needed: Varies based on activities chosen
Materials: Calendar, list of potential activities

This exercise helps couples intentionally build their shared experience bank:

Together, create three lists of potential shared experiences:

1. **Everyday Adventures**: Simple activities requiring minimal planning (trying a new restaurant, taking a different route on a walk, watching the sunset)

2. **Weekend Experiences**: Activities requiring moderate planning or resources (day trips, workshops, special events)

3. **Bucket List Adventures**: Significant experiences requiring more extensive planning (travel destinations, major life goals)

Schedule regular experience-building time:

- Weekly: Choose one item from the Everyday Adventures list

- Monthly: Select one item from the Weekend Experiences list 8.

- Annually: Plan progress toward one Bucket List Adventure

After each experience, take a few minutes to reflect together:
- What was your favorite moment?

- What did you learn about each other?

- What would you like to remember about this experience?

Document your experiences in a way that works for both of you—photos, journal entries, a special box for mementos, or simply the shared stories you'll tell later.

Spiritual Intimacy: Connecting Through Meaning and Purpose

Spiritual intimacy involves sharing and respecting each other's deepest values, beliefs about meaning and purpose, and approaches to life's existential questions. This dimension of intimacy doesn't require shared religious beliefs—it's about connecting around what gives your lives significance and how you make sense of the human experience.

Research shows that couples who can discuss spiritual matters openly, whether they share the same beliefs or not, report greater overall intimacy and relationship satisfaction.

The P.U.L.S.E. Approach to Spiritual Intimacy

Praise: Expressing appreciation for your partner's spiritual or philosophical perspective, even when it differs from your own. "I admire how your faith gives you such a strong foundation for helping others."

Understanding: Making the effort to comprehend your partner's spiritual framework without judgment or attempts to convert them to your viewpoint.

Listening: Creating space for open, non-defensive conversations about life's deeper questions.

Self-regulation: Managing potential reactivity when discussing topics where your spiritual or philosophical views differ.

Empathy: Connecting with the emotional and experiential aspects of your partner's spiritual life, even if you don't share their specific beliefs.

Exercise: Values and Meaning Exploration

Time needed: 60 minutes **Materials:** Paper and pens, comfortable setting This exercise helps couples explore their spiritual landscapes together:

Separately, reflect on and write about these questions:

- What gives your life the most meaning and purpose?

- What three values are most important to you, and why?

- How do you make sense of suffering or challenges in life?

- What practices help you feel connected to something larger than yourself?

- How have your spiritual or philosophical views evolved over time?

Come together and take turns sharing your reflections, with the listener practicing deep, non-judgmental attention. After each person shares, the listener asks curious, open-ended questions to deepen understanding rather than debating or trying to change the other's perspective.

Together, discuss:

- Where do our values and beliefs align?

- Where do they differ, and how can we honor those differences?

- How might we support each other's spiritual or philosophical growth?

- What shared practices or rituals might nurture our connection around meaning and purpose?

Physical Intimacy: The Language of Touch

Physical intimacy encompasses the full spectrum of physical connection—from casual affection like hand-holding and hugging to sexual intimacy. This dimension of connection allows us to express love, desire, playfulness, comfort, and care through our bodies.

In long-term relationships, maintaining a fulfilling physical connection requires intention and communication. Many couples find that physical intimacy naturally ebbs and flows, influenced by factors like stress, health, parenting demands, and relationship dynamics.

The P.U.L.S.E. Approach to Physical Intimacy

Praise: Expressing genuine appreciation for your partner's body, touch, and the ways they express physical affection. "I love how your touch always makes me feel both desired and safe."

Understanding: Recognizing that each person has unique needs and preferences around physical intimacy, influenced by their history, body image, stress levels, and more.

Listening: Being attentive to both verbal and non-verbal cues about your partner's physical needs and boundaries.

Self-regulation: Managing potential feelings of rejection or pressure around physical intimacy, allowing space for differences in desire or preference.

Empathy: Connecting with your partner's physical experience, which may be very different from your own due to gender, history, hormones, or other factors.

Exercise: Physical Connection Inventory

Time needed: 45-60 minutes **Materials:** Paper and pens, private comfortable setting.This exercise helps couples communicate about physical intimacy needs:
Separately, reflect on and write about:

- What forms of physical affection make you feel most loved and connected?

- What conditions help you feel most open to sexual intimacy?

- What barriers (internal or external) sometimes inhibit your desire for physical connection?

- What would you like more of in your physical relationship?

- What would you like less of or different in your physical relationship?

Come together and take turns sharing your reflections, with the listener practicing non-defensive listening. Together, create a "Physical Connection Plan" that includes:
- Daily affection rituals that meet both partners' needs

- Approaches to initiation that feel good to both partners

- Strategies for addressing common barriers to connection

- A commitment to regular check-ins about physical intimacy

Remember that this conversation is ongoing—physical needs and responses change over time and with life circumstances.

Balancing the Dimensions: Creating Your Unique Intimacy Profile

Every couple has a unique "intimacy profile"—their particular balance of connection across these five dimensions. There's no single "right" profile; what matters is that the pattern works for both partners and that no dimension is completely neglected.

Some couples might have especially strong intellectual and spiritual connection with moderate emphasis on the other dimensions. Others might prioritize emotional and physical intimacy with less focus on intellectual engagement. The key is finding a balance that feels fulfilling to both partners.

Exercise: Your Relationship Intimacy Profile
Time needed: 30-45 minutes **Materials:** Paper and pens
This exercise helps couples assess and enhance their intimacy balance:

Separately, rate your current satisfaction with each dimension of intimacy on a scale of 1-10:

- Emotional Intimacy

- Intellectual Intimacy

- Experiential Intimacy

- Spiritual Intimacy

- Physical Intimacy

Come together and share your ratings, discussing:
- Where are we strongest as a couple?

- Where might we benefit from more attention or growth?

- Are there significant differences in how we perceive our connection in any dimension?

Choose one dimension to focus on developing over the next month, creating a specific plan with activities from this chapter.

Schedule a follow-up conversation in one month to reassess and choose the next focus area.

Intimacy Across Life Transitions

Intimacy isn't static—it evolves as couples navigate life transitions like career changes, parenting, health challenges, or caring for aging parents. During these transitions, certain dimensions of intimacy may temporarily recede while others become more prominent.

For example, new parents often experience a temporary decrease in physical intimacy while their emotional and experiential connection deepens. Couples facing health challenges might find their spiritual intimacy growing even as physical connection requires adaptation.

The key is maintaining awareness of these natural shifts and communicating openly about them, rather than interpreting changes as signs of relationship problems. With intention and communication, couples can navigate these transitions while maintaining meaningful connection across the dimensions that are most accessible in each season.

Case Study: Intimacy Through Transition

When James received a cancer diagnosis at age 42, he and his wife Elena faced a profound challenge to their relationship. Treatment side effects significantly impacted their physical intimacy, and the emotional intensity of the experience sometimes made deep conversation difficult.

Rather than seeing these changes as relationship problems, they consciously adapted their intimacy focus. They developed new rituals of physical affection that worked within James's energy and comfort levels. They found that their spiritual connection deepened naturally as they faced mortality questions together.

They also discovered that experiential intimacy took on new importance—simple shared moments like watching a sunset or enjoying a favorite meal became profound connection points. By consciously attending to the dimensions of intimacy that were most accessible during this challenging time, they maintained their deep bond and even found that certain aspects of their connection strengthened through the crisis.

Dialogue Scripts:

Nurturing Multi-Dimensional Intimacy:

Here are examples of communication that fosters intimacy across dimensions:

For emotional intimacy: "I've been feeling anxious about this work situation, and I haven't shared it because I didn't want to burden you. But I realize keeping it to myself is actually creating distance between us. Could I share what I'm experiencing?"

For intellectual intimacy: "I found your perspective on that book really interesting— especially how you connected it to your own experiences. It made me think about it in a completely different way. What other insights did you have that we haven't discussed?"

For experiential intimacy: "I noticed how much you enjoyed that hiking trip last weekend. Your whole energy seemed different—more relaxed and playful. What was it about that experience that felt so good to you?"

For spiritual intimacy: "When you talked about finding meaning in your work, even on difficult days, it really resonated with me. I'd love to hear more about how your sense of purpose has evolved over the years."

For physical intimacy: "I've noticed that I feel most connected to you physically when we've had some time to talk and reconnect emotionally first. How about you—what helps you feel most open to physical connection?"

Chapter Reflection: Your Intimacy Journey

Take a moment to reflect on your current intimacy landscape:

1. Which dimension of intimacy feels strongest in your relationship right now?

2. Which dimension would you most like to develop further, and why?

3. What's one barrier to deeper intimacy that you personally bring to the relationship (e.g., fear of vulnerability, difficulty expressing needs, etc.)?

4. What's one specific action you could take this week to foster deeper connection in your relationship?

5. How might you use the P.U.L.S.E. framework to enhance intimacy across all dimensions?

The Bridge to the Next Chapter: From Intimacy to Shared Vision

Deep intimacy across these five dimensions creates the foundation for another crucial aspect of thriving relationships: a shared vision for your life together. When you're deeply connected emotionally, intellectually, experientially, spiritually, and physically, you're better equipped to create and pursue meaningful shared goals and dreams.

In the next chapter, we'll explore how to develop this shared vision—how to align your individual hopes and dreams into a compelling picture of your future together that honors both your unique identities and your partnership. You'll discover how the P.U.L.S.E. framework can help you navigate differences in priorities and create a life path that feels fulfilling to both of you.

But before we move on, I encourage you to begin practicing the intimacy-building exercises in this chapter. Remember that intimacy deepens gradually through consistent small moments of connection rather than grand gestures. Each time you make the effort to connect more deeply across any dimension, you strengthen the foundation of your relationship and create greater capacity for joy, resilience, and meaning in your shared life.

LOVE WITH P.U.L.S.E.

KEEP GOING AFTER THE CHAPTER ENDS

- Guided Video Exercises
- Printable Worksheets
- Real-Life Tools You Can Use Today

Turn what you just read into what you can actually do — right now.

Dr. Ashley R. Bryant

Creator of the P.U.L.S.E. Framework & Author of Love With P.U.L.S.E.

Already finished the book? Scan to access every chapter's bonus content in one place.

Chapter 9
Building a Shared Vision

Every great achievement begins with a vision—a compelling image of what could be. This is as true for relationships as it is for businesses, artistic endeavors, or social movements. Couples who thrive over the long term don't just drift through life together; they consciously create and pursue a shared vision that gives their relationship purpose, direction, and meaning.

In this chapter, we'll explore how to develop a compelling shared vision for your relationship and life together—one that honors both your individual dreams and your collective aspirations. We'll discover how the P.U.L.S.E. framework can help you navigate differences in priorities and create a life path that feels deeply fulfilling to both partners.

The Power of Shared Vision in Relationships

A shared vision serves several crucial functions in a thriving relationship:

1. Direction and Purpose: It provides a north star that guides your decisions, both big and small, giving your relationship a sense of forward momentum.

2. Meaning and Significance: It connects your daily actions and choices to something larger, infusing ordinary moments with deeper meaning.

3. Resilience Through Challenges: When difficulties arise, a compelling shared vision reminds you why the struggle matters and helps you persevere.

4. Alignment and Synergy: It helps you coordinate your efforts and resources toward common goals, creating greater impact than either could achieve alone.

5. Growth and Evolution: A well-crafted vision inspires ongoing development, both individually and as a couple.

Research in relationship psychology confirms that couples who create and maintain a sense of shared meaning and purpose report higher relationship satisfaction, greater resilience during challenges, and more effective problem-solving.

Case Study: The Vision Vacuum

After fifteen years of marriage, Tomas and Leila found themselves in what they called a "vision vacuum." Their early years together had been driven by clear shared goals—completing their education, establishing careers, buying a home, and raising their children. With these milestones achieved and their children now teenagers, they realized they hadn't developed new shared dreams to carry them forward.

This absence of compelling future vision left them feeling disconnected and uncertain.

Their conversations revolved around logistics and problems rather than possibilities and aspirations. Without a shared sense of where they were heading together, they began drifting in different directions—Tomas throwing himself into work projects and Leila focusing on her newly discovered passion for community activism.

Through couples therapy, they realized they needed to intentionally create a new shared vision for their next chapter. The process of exploring their individual dreams and weaving them into a compelling shared future reconnected them emotionally and intellectually. Their new vision—centered around travel, creative pursuits, and mentoring younger couples—gave them renewed energy and purpose, both individually and as a team.

The P.U.L.S.E. Approach to Creating Shared Vision

The P.U.L.S.E. framework provides powerful tools for developing a vision that truly resonates with both partners:

Praise: Acknowledging and celebrating each other's dreams and aspirations creates safety for authentic sharing. "I love how passionate you are about that goal—your enthusiasm is inspiring."

Understanding: Making the effort to comprehend not just what your partner wants but why it matters to them—the values and needs underlying their dreams.

Listening: Creating space for each partner to fully express their hopes and vision without immediate evaluation or problem-solving.

Self-regulation: Managing potential disappointment or anxiety when your partner's vision differs from yours, allowing space for exploration before seeking compromise.

Empathy: Connecting emotionally with what your partner's dreams mean to them, even when they're different from your own priorities.

The Vision Creation Process: From Individual Dreams to Shared Purpose

Creating a compelling shared vision is both an art and a science. The following structured process helps couples move from individual aspirations to a unified vision that energizes both partners:

Step 1: Individual Vision Exploration

Before attempting to create a shared vision, each partner needs clarity about their own dreams and aspirations. This prevents the common pitfall of one partner subordinating their desires to the other's vision.

Exercise: Personal Vision Mapping

Time needed: 60-90 minutes **Materials**: Journal or paper, pens, optional vision board materials (magazines, scissors, glue, poster board)

Working separately, each partner explores these questions:

- Life Areas Exploration: For each key life area (career/purpose, health/wellbeing, relationships, personal growth, leisure/play, contribution/legacy), reflect on:

    - What would bring you the most fulfillment in this area over the next 3-5 years?

    - What values are most important to you in this area?

    - What changes would you like to see from your current situation?

- Visualization: Imagine waking up 3-5 years from now on an ideal day:

    - Where are you?

    - Who is with you?

    - What are you doing?

    - How do you feel?

    - What are you most proud of having

accomplished? Write a detailed description of this day as if it's already happening.

- Essence Identification: Review what you've written and identify:

    - What themes emerge across different life areas?

    - What core values are expressed in your vision?

    - What 3-5 elements feel most essential to your fulfillment?

This individual exploration creates the foundation for meaningful shared vision work. By clarifying your own aspirations first, you bring your authentic self to the partnership visioning process.

Step 2: Compassionate Vision Sharing

Once each partner has clarity about their individual vision elements, the next step is to share these with each other in a structured, supportive way.

Exercise: Vision Exchange
Time needed: 90 minutes (may be split into multiple sessions) **Materials**: Individual vision notes from previous exercise, fresh paper for notes

Create a Supportive Environment: Choose a time when you're both relaxed and not rushed. Create a pleasant atmosphere free from distractions.

Set Sharing Guidelines:
- One person shares at a time without interruption
- The listener practices deep curiosity without judgment
- No problem-solving or reality-checking during the sharing phase
- Focus on understanding the meaning and values behind each element

Structured Sharing Process:
- Partner A shares their vision for one life area (10 minutes)
- Partner B asks curious questions to deepen understanding (5 minutes)
- Partner B reflects back what they heard, focusing on the values and meaning (3 minutes)
- Switch roles and repeat for Partner B's vision in the same life area
- Continue until all life areas have been explored

Capture Insights: After completing the exchange, each partner notes:

- What surprised you about your partner's vision?

- What elements resonated most strongly with your own vision?

- What values do you clearly share?

- Where do you see potential challenges in alignment?

This compassionate exchange creates mutual understanding of each other's aspirations without immediately jumping to evaluation or compromise. It honors the integrity of each person's dreams while building the foundation for integration.

Step 3: Finding the Intersection

With a clear understanding of both individual visions, couples can now identify areas of natural alignment and creative integration.

Exercise: Vision Mapping
Time needed: 60 minutes **Materials**: Large paper or whiteboard, colored markers
Create a Visual Map:
- Draw a large Venn diagram with two overlapping circles

- In the left circle, place elements unique to Partner

A's vision

- In the right circle, place elements unique to Partner B's vision

- In the overlapping center, place elements that are already aligned or compatible

Identify Shared Values: On a separate sheet, list the core values that emerged from both visions. Circle those that are shared or complementary.

Explore Integration Possibilities: For elements that initially seem in conflict, discuss:

- What core need or value underlies this element for each person?

- Are there ways to meet both sets of needs through creative alternatives?

- Could these elements be pursued in different time frames rather than simultaneously?

- Might some elements be pursued individually while supporting each other?

Draft Integration Statements: For each major life area, create a statement that captures an integrated vision that honors both partners' core needs and values.

This mapping process helps couples visualize where their visions naturally align and where creative integration is needed. It transforms the conversation from "your vision versus my vision" to "our shared vision that honors both of us."

Step 4: Crafting Your Relationship Vision Statement

The final step is creating a concise, inspiring vision statement that captures the essence of your shared future.

> **Exercise: Vision Statement Creation**
> **Time needed**: 45-60 minutes **Materials:** Paper, pens, final version on special paper if desired
> Review Your Integration Work: Look back at your vision mapping and integration statements, noting the themes and elements that feel most energizing and meaningful to both of you.
> Draft Individual Versions: Separately, each partner writes a 1-2 paragraph vision statement that captures what you want to create together over the next 3-5 years.
> Share and Integrate:
> - Read your drafts aloud to each other
> - Highlight phrases or elements from each that resonate strongly
> - Together, craft a unified statement that incorporates the best elements from both drafts
>
> Refine for Impact: The most powerful vision statements are:

- Concise (1-2 paragraphs)

- Written in present tense, as if already happening

- Emotionally evocative

- Specific enough to guide decisions but flexible enough to adapt

- Reflective of both partners' values and aspirations

Create a Visible Reminder: Write your vision statement somewhere special— perhaps framed on your wall, in a journal you both contribute to, or as the screensaver on your devices.

Example Vision Statement:

"Our relationship is a vibrant partnership where we both continue to grow individually while creating a life of adventure, meaning, and deep connection together. We prioritize experiences over possessions, making time for both local explorations and international travel that broadens our perspectives and creates lasting memories.

We nurture a home that serves as both a peaceful sanctuary and a welcoming gathering place for friends and family. Our work reflects our values of creativity and service, with Michelle's writing career flourishing alongside David's community development projects. We support each other's personal passions while maintaining rich connection through daily rituals of presence and weekly adventures. Our relationship serves as both our anchor and our wings, providing the security to take risks and the freedom to evolve."

From Vision to Reality: Implementation Strategies

A beautiful vision remains just a dream unless coupled with practical implementation.

These strategies help couples translate their vision into daily reality:

1. Create a Vision-Aligned Decision Filter

Develop a simple set of questions to evaluate opportunities and decisions against your vision:

- Does this choice move us toward or away from our vision?
- Does this honor both our individual and shared priorities?
- Will we be glad we made this choice when we look back in five years?

Using this filter helps ensure daily decisions align with your longer-term aspirations.

2. Establish Vision-Supporting Rituals

Design regular practices that reinforce your vision:

- Daily Connection Points: Brief check-ins that remind you of your shared purpose
- Weekly Planning Sessions: Time to coordinate schedules and priorities in alignment with vision
- Monthly Vision Dates: Deeper conversations about progress and adjustments needed
- Annual Vision Retreats: Extended time to reflect, celebrate progress, and refine your vision

3. Create Accountability Structures

Identify ways to keep your vision active and present:

- Share your vision with trusted friends who can provide supportive accountability
- Set calendar reminders for vision- related check-ins
- Create visual reminders in your home or workspace
- Develop metrics or milestones to track progress on key vision elements

4. Balance Structure and Flexibility

Remember that vision implementation requires both structure and adaptability:

- Use structure to maintain momentum and overcome inertia

- Maintain flexibility to adapt to changing circumstances and evolving desires

- View your vision as a living document that guides rather than constrains

Case Study: Vision in Action

When Maya and James created their shared vision centered around a location- independent lifestyle that would allow them to live internationally while maintaining their careers, they knew implementation would require careful planning.

They established a three-year timeline, breaking it into specific milestones: developing remote work skills, reducing possessions, building savings, researching visa requirements, and creating passive income streams.

Their vision influenced daily decisions—from declining a promotion that would require more office presence to investing in language learning instead of home renovations.

They established weekly planning sessions to coordinate their efforts and quarterly "vision weekends" to assess progress and make adjustments.

When unexpected challenges arose—like a family health crisis that delayed their timeline—their clear vision helped *them adapt without abandoning their dream. Three and a half years later, they achieved their goal of location independence, beginning with a six-month stay in Portugal while maintaining their professional responsibilities remotely.*

Their success came not just from having a compelling vision, but from the consistent, coordinated actions they took to bring it to life.

Navigating Vision Differences and Conflicts

Even with the best process, couples will encounter areas where their visions differ significantly. These differences aren't necessarily problems—they can be opportunities for growth and creativity—but they require skillful navigation.

Common Vision Conflicts and Solutions

1. Different Timelines Conflict: One partner wants to pursue a vision element immediately while the other prefers to wait. Solution: Create a phased approach that honors both timing needs—perhaps starting with a smaller version now while building toward the fuller vision over time.

2. Resource Allocation Differences Conflict: Partners prioritize different uses for limited resources like money, time, or energy. Solution: Create a resource allocation plan that ensures both partners' priority vision elements receive support, even if not equally at all times.

3. Location Disagreements Conflict: Partners feel drawn to different geographical locations for living or career opportunities. Solution: Explore creative alternatives like splitting time between locations, time-limited compromises with planned reevaluation, or finding a third location that meets core needs of both.

4. Relationship Structure Differences Conflict: Partners have different visions for relationship elements like parenting, division of responsibilities, or social connections.

Solution: Focus on the underlying needs and values rather than specific forms, then co- create new approaches that honor both sets of needs.

Dialogue Example: Navigating Vision Differences

Partner A: "I'm feeling torn because my career vision really requires being in a major city, but I know your vision includes more space and connection with nature."

Partner B: "That does seem like a real tension point. I'm curious though—what is it about the city that feels essential for your career vision?"

Partner A: "It's really about access to the industry network, collaborative opportunities, and being able to attend key events. I worry I'd miss important connections if we were too far away."

Partner B: "And for me, having outdoor space and quieter surroundings feels necessary for my wellbeing and creative work. I wonder if there might be options we haven't considered that could address both needs?"

Partner A: "Maybe we could look at areas that are within commuting distance of the city but still have more space and natural surroundings? Or perhaps I could arrange to be in the city intensively for certain periods while basing our home somewhere that better supports your needs?"

Partner B: "I like both those ideas. What if we made a list of our non-negotiable needs for location and then researched areas that might meet those core requirements, even if they're not our initial vision of either 'city' or 'country'?"

This dialogue demonstrates how focusing on underlying needs rather than fixed positions opens space for creative solutions that honor both partners' core vision elements.

Evolving Your Vision: The Ongoing Journey

A relationship vision isn't a static document but an evolving expression of your shared journey. Life changes, unexpected opportunities arise, and personal growth shifts priorities. Healthy couples revisit and refresh their vision regularly.

Signs Your Vision Needs Refreshing:

One or both partners feel a lack of energy or enthusiasm about current goals Major life transitions have occurred (career changes, children leaving home, health challenges) You've achieved significant vision elements and haven't created new aspirations

External circumstances have dramatically changed your options or priorities

One partner feels their evolving values or desires aren't reflected in the current vision

Exercise: The Vision Refresh Process
Time needed: 2-3 hours **Materials:** Your current vision statement, journal or paper, pens
Appreciative Review: Begin by acknowledging what's working in your current vision and what you've accomplished together.
Individual Reflection: Separately, consider:
- What elements of our vision still energize and inspire me?

- What feels outdated or no longer aligned with who I am becoming?

- What new aspirations or values have emerged for me?

Compassionate Sharing: Share your reflections using the same structured process from the Vision Exchange exercise.

Integration and Updating: Together, update your vision statement to reflect your current values, circumstances, and aspirations.

Recommitment Ritual: Create a simple ritual to mark your refreshed vision—perhaps a special dinner, a symbolic action, or sharing your updated vision with trusted friends.

Dialogue Scripts: Vision-Building Conversations

Here are examples of language that facilitates effective vision-building:

- When exploring individual aspirations: "I'd love to understand more about why that goal matters so deeply to you. What values or experiences have shaped that dream?"

- When acknowledging differences: "I can see our visions differ in this area. I'm curious if we could explore the underlying needs or values that make this important to each of us, rather than focusing just on the specific form."

- When seeking integration: "What if we look for a third option that isn't exactly what either of us initially pictured, but might honor what matters most to both of us?"

- When making vision-aligned decisions: "Before we decide, let's check this option against our shared vision. Does this choice move us toward the life we've said we want to create together?"

- When celebrating vision progress: "I want to acknowledge how this experience/achievement aligns with the vision we created together. I feel proud of how we're bringing our dreams to life."

Chapter Reflection: Your Vision Journey

Take a moment to reflect on your current relationship vision:

1. Do you and your partner have an explicit, shared vision for your life together? If not, what has prevented you from creating one?

2. How aligned do you feel your individual aspirations are with your shared path?

3. What processes or conversations have been most helpful in creating shared direction in your relationship?

4. What's one element of your vision that energizes you both when you think about it?

5. What's one step you could take this week to bring your vision more fully into your daily life?

The Bridge to the Next Chapter: From Vision to Resilience

A compelling shared vision provides direction and meaning for your relationship journey. However, every meaningful journey includes challenges and setbacks. In the next chapter, we'll explore how to cultivate resilience as a couple—the ability to navigate difficulties while maintaining connection and continuing to move toward your shared vision. We'll discover how the P.U.L.S.E. framework helps couples not just survive challenges but grow stronger through them, transforming potential relationship threats into opportunities for deeper connection and shared strength. But before we move on, I encourage you to begin the vision-building exercises in this chapter. Remember that creating a shared vision is not a one-time event but an ongoing conversation. Each time you engage in this process, you strengthen your sense of partnership and purpose, creating a relationship that is not just loving but also meaningful and directional.

LOVE WITH P.U.L.S.E.

KEEP GOING AFTER THE CHAPTER ENDS

- Guided Video Exercises
- Printable Worksheets
- Real-Life Tools You Can Use Today

Turn what you just read into what you can actually do — right now.

Dr. Ashley R. Bryant

Creator of the P.U.L.S.E. Framework & Author of Love With P.U.L.S.E.

Already finished the book? Scan to access every chapter's bonus content in one place.

CHAPTER 10
Cultivating Resilience as a Couple

Every relationship faces challenges. From everyday stressors like work pressure and financial concerns to major life transitions and unexpected crises, the journey of partnership inevitably includes difficult terrain. What distinguishes relationships that thrive over the long term isn't an absence of challenges but rather the capacity to navigate these challenges while maintaining connection and even growing stronger through them. This capacity is what we call relationship resilience.

In this chapter, we'll explore how to cultivate resilience as a couple—how to build the strength, flexibility, and resources that allow your relationship to withstand stress, recover from difficulties, and adapt to change. We'll discover how the P.U.L.S.E. framework provides powerful tools for developing this essential quality, transforming potential relationship threats into opportunities for deeper connection.

Understanding Relationship Resilience

Resilience in relationships has three key components:

- Resistance: The ability to withstand stress without significant damage to the relationship—like a well-built house that remains standing during strong winds.

- Recovery: The capacity to bounce back from difficulties and return to a state of connection and functioning—like a tree that bends in a storm but returns to its original position afterward.

- Reconfiguration: The ability to adapt and grow in response to challenges, sometimes emerging stronger than before—like a community that rebuilds after a disaster with improved infrastructure and stronger bonds.

- Research shows that resilient couples don't just endure challenges—they often experience what psychologists call "stress-related growth," finding that navigating difficulties together actually strengthens their bond and deepens their connection.

Case Study: From Crisis to Connection

When Sophia was diagnosed with a chronic illness in their fifth year of marriage, she and her husband Marcus faced a profound challenge to their relationship. The diagnosis required significant lifestyle changes, altered their financial plans, and impacted their dreams of starting a family.

Initially, they struggled. Marcus felt helpless in the face of Sophia's pain and withdrew emotionally, while Sophia feared becoming a burden and tried to manage everything herself. Their communication broke down, and they found themselves drifting apart precisely when they needed each other most.

Through couples therapy, they learned to approach this challenge differently. Marcus found ways to offer meaningful support without trying to "fix" the unfixable. Sophia learned to express her needs clearly and accept help. Together, they developed new rituals of connection adapted to their changed circumstances.

Three years later, they described the illness as something that had ultimately strengthened their relationship. "We know we can face hard things together now,"

Marcus explained. "We've developed a level of communication and teamwork we never had before." Sophia added, "I never wanted this illness, but I'm grateful for how it's deepened our connection. We don't take each other for granted anymore."

Their experience illustrates how couples can not just survive challenges but grow through them, developing greater resilience for whatever comes next.

The P.U.L.S.E. Approach to Relationship Resilience

The five elements of the P.U.L.S.E. framework provide powerful tools for building relationship resilience:

Praise: Maintaining appreciation and positive regard, especially during difficult times, creates an emotional buffer that helps relationships withstand stress.

Understanding: Seeking to comprehend each partner's unique experience of challenges prevents misunderstandings and alienation during stressful periods.

Listening: Creating space for each partner to express their concerns, fears, and needs during difficulties ensures both feel seen and supported.

Self-regulation: Managing individual stress responses prevents the escalation of tension and allows for thoughtful rather than reactive responses to challenges.

Empathy: Connecting with each other's emotional experience during hardship creates a profound sense of "we're in this together" that is the essence of resilience.

Building Your Relationship Resilience Toolkit

Just as individuals can develop personal resilience through specific practices, couples can intentionally build relationship resilience. The following strategies create a comprehensive toolkit for navigating life's inevitable challenges:

1. Cultivate a Stress-Buffering Narrative

The stories we tell about our relationship—particularly during difficult times— profoundly impact our resilience. Couples who frame challenges as "us against the problem" rather than "you versus me" are significantly more resilient.

Exercise: Creating Your Resilience Story
Time needed: 45-60 minutes **Materials**: Journal or paper, pens

Together, identify a challenge you've successfully navigated as a couple.

Separately, write your individual accounts of this experience, focusing on:

- How you worked together to face the challenge

- Strengths each of you brought to the situation

- What you learned about yourselves and each other

- How the experience affected your relationship

Share your stories with each other, noting similarities and differences in your perceptions.

Together, create a unified "resilience story" that captures how you faced this challenge as a team.

Discuss how this narrative might inform how you approach future challenges.

This exercise helps couples develop what researchers call a "couple identity"—a sense of themselves as a unified team that can face difficulties together. This shared identity is a powerful resilience factor.

2. Build Your Stress Communication Protocol

Many couples communicate less effectively precisely when clear communication is most needed—during times of stress. Developing a shared understanding of how each partner experiences and expresses stress, along with agreed-upon communication strategies, creates a foundation for resilience.

3. Develop Resilience Rituals

Intentional rituals help relationships maintain connection and stability during turbulent times. These rituals serve as anchors, providing predictability and reassurance when other aspects of life feel chaotic.

Types of Resilience Rituals:

Daily Connection Rituals: Brief but meaningful interactions that maintain your emotional bond.

- A six-second kiss when leaving or returning home
- A daily check-in where each partner shares a high point and challenge
- A bedtime gratitude practice where you each share something you appreciate about the other

Stress-Response Rituals:

Specific practices you engage in when facing difficulties.

- A weekly "state of the union" conversation during challenging periods

- A shared physical activity that helps release tension

- A specific phrase or gesture that signals "I'm here with you in this"

Celebration Rituals:

Ways of acknowledging progress and small victories, even amid larger challenges.

- Weekly recognition of "wins" no matter how small

- Monthly reflection on what you're learning and how you're growing through challenges

- Marking significant milestones in your resilience journey

Exercise: Designing Your Resilience Rituals
Time needed: 30 minutes **Materials**: Paper and pens
Together, brainstorm potential rituals for each category above, considering what would feel meaningful and sustainable for your specific relationship.
Select at least one ritual from each category to implement immediately.

Create a plan for when and how you'll practice these rituals, being specific about timing and responsibilities. Schedule a one-month check-in to assess how these rituals are working and make adjustments as needed.

4. Build Your Support Network

No couple is an island. Research consistently shows that couples with strong social support networks demonstrate greater resilience during challenges. These networks provide practical assistance, emotional support, perspective, and models of resilience.

> **Exercise: Mapping Your Relationship Support System**
> **Time needed:** 45 minutes **Materials**: Large paper, colored markers
> Draw a large circle in the center of the paper representing your relationship.
> Around this circle, identify and map different sources of support:
> - Individual friends who support your relationship
> - Couples whose relationships you admire
> - Family members who understand and encourage your partnership
> - Communities you belong to (religious, interest-based, neighborhood)

- Professional resources (therapists, coaches, financial advisors)

For each support source, note what specific types of support they provide:
- Emotional support

- Practical assistance

- Wisdom/guidance

- Role modeling

- Fun/stress relief

Identify any gaps in your support system and discuss how you might strengthen these areas.
Create a plan for intentionally nurturing these supportive connections, especially during challenging periods.

5. Develop Financial Resilience

Financial stress is consistently rated among the top relationship stressors. Building financial resilience—not just through wealth accumulation but through shared values, communication, and planning—significantly enhances overall relationship resilience.

Exercise: Financial Resilience Planning

Time needed: 60-90 minutes (may be split into multiple sessions) **Materials**: Financial documents, paper and pens
Together, assess your current financial resilience by discussing:

- Do we have an emergency fund that covers 3-6 months of expenses?

- Do we have a budget that reflects our shared values and priorities?

- Do we have insurance coverage appropriate to our situation?

- Do we have a plan for managing debt?

- Do we have regular financial check-ins to stay aligned?

Identify your top three financial vulnerabilities as a couple.
Create a specific plan to address each vulnerability, with clear action steps and timelines.
Establish a regular financial communication ritual—perhaps a monthly "money date" where you review your situation and progress toward goals in a relaxed, nonjudgmental setting.
Consider consulting with a financial advisor who can provide objective guidance tailored to your specific situation.

Navigating Specific Relationship Challenges

While the resilience strategies above apply broadly, certain challenges benefit from specific approaches. Here's guidance for navigating some common relationship stressors:

Career Transitions and Work Stress

Work-related challenges—whether job loss, career changes, or ongoing work stress—can significantly impact relationships. Resilient couples approach these challenges as a team while respecting individual career needs.

Resilience Strategies:

Compartmentalization Skills: Learn to create boundaries between work stress and relationship time, perhaps through transition rituals when coming home.

Role Flexibility: Be willing to adjust household responsibilities when one partner's work demands increase temporarily.

Career Support Without Enmeshment: Show interest and support for your partner's career without taking their work challenges personally or trying to solve all their professional problems.

Shared Meaning Around Work: Discuss how each of your careers connects to your larger values and relationship vision, helping maintain perspective during difficult periods.

Parenting Challenges

For couples with children, parenting stressors can significantly impact the relationship.

From sleep deprivation with newborns to navigating teen challenges, parenting requires ongoing adaptation and teamwork.

Resilience Strategies:

Parenting Partnership: Develop explicit agreements about parenting approaches and division of responsibilities, updating these as children's needs evolve.

Protect Couple Time: Maintain regular couple-focused time, even if brief, rather than functioning solely as co-parents.

United Front With Flexibility: Present consistency to children while maintaining private space to discuss differences in parenting approaches.

Mutual Respite: Ensure both partners get breaks from parenting demands, supporting each other's need for rest and rejuvenation.

Health Challenges

Whether acute or chronic, health issues create significant relationship stress. The partner with health concerns may struggle with dependency and identity changes, while the supporting partner may experience caregiver burden and helplessness.

Resilience Strategies:

Maintain Identity Beyond Illness/Caregiving: Actively work to ensure that health challenges don't completely define either partner or the relationship.

Calibrate Support: Discuss what types of support feel helpful versus what might inadvertently foster dependency or resentment.

Acknowledge Grief: Create space to acknowledge losses associated with health changes while also adapting expectations and finding new sources of meaning.

Seek Outside Support: Utilize professional and community resources rather than expecting the relationship to meet all practical and emotional needs during health challenges.

Extended Family Tensions

Difficulties with in-laws or other family members can create significant relationship stress, especially when partners have different perspectives on family boundaries or obligations.

Resilience Strategies:

Prioritize Your Partnership: Make explicit agreements about putting your relationship first, even when navigating complex family dynamics.

Develop Clear Boundaries: Create shared understanding about what information is shared with extended family, how much influence family members have on decisions, and how you'll handle family conflicts.

Support Without Agreement: Learn to support each other in family relationships even when you don't fully understand or agree with your partner's family dynamics.

United Communication: Present a united front in communications with extended family while maintaining space for different individual relationships.

Recovering from Relationship Injuries

Even the most resilient relationships sometimes experience significant injuries—betrayals, periods of neglect, or other wounds that damage trust and connection. The ability to heal from these injuries is a crucial aspect of relationship resilience.

The Healing Process

Research on relationship recovery suggests a four-stage process for healing significant injuries:

- Acknowledgment: The partner who caused the injury fully acknowledges the impact of their actions without defensiveness or minimization.

- Attunement: Both partners work to understand the

deeper meaning of the injury, including how it connected to existing vulnerabilities or past wounds.

- Apology: The injuring partner offers a complete apology that takes full responsibility and expresses genuine remorse.

- Amends: The couple works together to rebuild trust through consistent actions over time, creating a new relationship narrative that incorporates but is not defined by the injury.

Exercise: Healing Dialogue for Relationship Injuries
Time needed: 60-90 minutes (may require multiple sessions) **Materials**: Private, comfortable space; tissues
For significant relationship injuries, this structured dialogue helps facilitate healing:
Setting the Stage:
- Choose a time when both partners can be fully present

- Agree to focus on understanding rather than defending

- Commit to using time-outs if the conversation becomes too intense

Injury Expression:
- The hurt partner expresses their experience using "I" statements

- They share not just what happened but how it affected them emotionally

- They connect this to deeper meanings or past experiences that intensified the impact

Empathic Listening:
- The other partner listens without interrupting or defending

- They focus on understanding their partner's emotional experience

- They reflect back what they're hearing to confirm understanding

Responsibility Taking:
- The partner who caused the injury acknowledges their actions and impact

- They express genuine remorse without qualifications or excuses

- They share their understanding of why this was hurtful to their partner

Moving Forward:
- Together, discuss specific actions that would help rebuild trust

- Create agreements about how to prevent similar injuries in the future

- Acknowledge that healing is a process that takes time and consistent effort

For major relationship injuries like infidelity or significant breaches of trust, professional support from a couples therapist is often beneficial in facilitating this healing process.

Building Post-Traumatic Growth Together

Psychologists have identified a phenomenon called "post-traumatic growth"—the positive psychological changes that can emerge from the struggle with highly challenging life circumstances. This concept applies not just to individuals but to relationships as well.

Couples who navigate significant challenges together often report that their relationship actually strengthened through the process, developing:

- Greater appreciation for each other and life in general
- Deeper emotional connection and intimacy
- Enhanced sense of personal and relationship strength
- New possibilities and directions they hadn't previously considered
- Spiritual or existential growth and deeper sense of

meaning

Exercise: Identifying Growth Through Challenges
Time needed: 45-60 minutes **Materials**: Journal or paper, pens

This exercise helps couples recognize and build upon the growth that can emerge from difficulties:

- Together, identify a significant challenge you've faced as a couple.

- Separately, reflect on and write about:

- How has this challenge changed you individually?

- How has it changed your perspective on your relationship?

- What strengths or capacities have you developed through this experience?

- What do you appreciate more deeply now than before?

- What new possibilities have emerged from this challenge?

- Share your reflections with each other, listening for themes and connections.

Together, discuss:

- How might we intentionally build on this growth?

- How can we incorporate what we've learned into our relationship moving forward?

- How might this growth prepare us for future challenges?

Create a symbolic way to acknowledge this growth—perhaps a small ritual, a meaningful object, or a written statement that captures what you've gained through this challenge.

Dialogue Scripts: Resilience in Conversation

Here are examples of communication that fosters resilience during challenging times:

When facing a new challenge: "This is really difficult, but I believe in us. We've navigated hard things before, and we'll find our way through this together too."

When offering support: "I can see how much you're struggling with this. What would feel most supportive right now? Do you need me to listen, to help problem-solve, or maybe just to sit with you for a while?"

When feeling overwhelmed: "I'm feeling really overwhelmed by everything that's happening. I need some time to process, but I want you to know this isn't about us—I'm not pulling away from you, just trying to get my bearings."

When acknowledging growth: "Looking back, I can see how much stronger we've become through this challenge. I've been especially moved by how you've [specific quality or action], and I think we've developed a deeper trust in our ability to face things together."

When requesting a resilience check-in: "We've been in the thick of this situation for a while now. Could we take some time this weekend to check in about how we're doing—not just about the practical aspects, but how we're feeling about us and how we're supporting each other?"

Chapter Reflection: Your Resilience Journey

Take a moment to reflect on your relationship's resilience capacity:

1. What challenges have you successfully navigated together, and what did these experiences teach you about your strengths as a couple?

2. What current or anticipated challenges might test your relationship resilience?

3. Which resilience strategies from this chapter seem most relevant to your specific situation?

4. What resilience rituals could you implement to strengthen your connection during difficult times?

5. How might you support each other's individual

resilience while also building your capacity as a couple?

The Bridge to the Next Chapter: From Resilience to Celebration

While this chapter has focused on navigating challenges, a truly thriving relationship balances resilience with celebration. In the next chapter, we'll explore the importance of celebrating wins—both large and small—and how the P.U.L.S.E. framework can help you create a relationship culture that acknowledges progress, expresses gratitude, and savors positive experiences.

We'll discover how intentional celebration enhances relationship satisfaction, builds emotional reserves for challenging times, and reinforces the behaviors and connections that matter most to both partners.

But before we move on, I encourage you to begin implementing the resilience-building exercises in this chapter. Remember that relationship resilience, like physical strength, develops through consistent practice rather than in a single effort. Each time you intentionally apply these strategies, you're building your capacity to not just weather life's inevitable storms but to grow stronger through them, creating a relationship that becomes more robust and deeply connected with each challenge you face together.

LOVE WITH P.U.L.S.E.

KEEP GOING AFTER THE CHAPTER ENDS

- Guided Video Exercises
- Printable Worksheets
- Real-Life Tools You Can Use Today

Turn what you just read into what you can actually do — right now.

Dr. Ashley R. Bryant

Creator of the P.U.L.S.E. Framework & Author of Love With P.U.L.S.E.

Already finished the book? Scan to access every chapter's bonus content in one place.

Chapter 11
Celebrating Wins: The Art of Savoring Success Together

In our quest to build stronger relationships, we often focus on solving problems, navigating conflicts, and overcoming challenges. While these skills are essential, equally important—yet frequently overlooked—is the practice of celebrating wins together. The ability to acknowledge, appreciate, and savor positive experiences is not just a pleasant addition to your relationship; research shows it's a fundamental component of lasting relationship satisfaction and resilience.

In this chapter, we'll explore how to cultivate a celebration mindset in your relationship—how to notice, amplify, and commemorate both significant achievements and everyday moments of connection. We'll discover how the P.U.L.S.E. framework can enhance your capacity to experience joy together, creating a relationship that doesn't just weather difficulties but truly thrives.

The Science of Celebration in Relationships

Relationship research reveals something fascinating: the ratio of positive to negative interactions is a powerful predictor of relationship success. Dr. John Gottman's groundbreaking studies found that thriving relationships maintain a ratio of at least 5:1—five positive interactions for every negative one. In contrast, relationships headed for trouble typically have ratios closer to 1:1 or worse.

This "magic ratio" highlights why celebration matters so much. When couples intentionally create and savor positive moments together, they build an emotional bank account that helps buffer against inevitable conflicts and stresses. These positive experiences aren't just pleasant diversions—they're essential investments in the relationship's long-term health.

Neuroscience adds another dimension to this understanding. When we celebrate together, our brains release neurochemicals like oxytocin (the bonding hormone), dopamine (associated with pleasure and reward), and endorphins (natural mood elevators). These biological responses strengthen our attachment bonds and create positive associations with our relationship, making us more likely to turn toward each other during difficult times.

Case Study: The Celebration Deficit

After seven years together, Maya and James realized their relationship had fallen into a troubling pattern. They were excellent problem-solvers, efficiently addressing household tasks, financial decisions, and parenting challenges. But somewhere along the way, they'd stopped celebrating together.

Achievements at work were acknowledged with a quick "congrats" before moving on to the next task. Relationship milestones passed unnoticed. Even vacations felt more like items to check off their to-do list than opportunities to connect and create joyful memories.

In couples therapy, they discovered this "celebration deficit" was draining their relationship of vitality. While they hadn't developed major problems, they'd lost the spark that made their relationship energizing and meaningful. Their therapist helped them see that their efficiency-focused approach to life, while productive, was robbing them of opportunities to build positive emotional connections.

By intentionally incorporating celebration practices—from elaborate acknowledgments of major achievements to brief daily appreciation rituals—they gradually shifted their relationship culture. Six months later, both reported feeling more connected, more appreciative of each other, and more aware of the good in their lives together.

The P.U.L.S.E. Approach to Celebration

The five elements of the P.U.L.S.E. framework provide powerful tools for enhancing your capacity to celebrate together:

Praise: Expressing specific, genuine appreciation for your partner's qualities and actions creates opportunities for shared positive emotion.

Understanding: Recognizing what types of acknowledgment and celebration are most meaningful to your specific partner allows you to celebrate in ways that truly resonate.

Listening: Being fully present to hear about your partner's joys and successes—rather than competing, minimizing, or quickly changing the subject—allows for deeper connection through shared positive experiences.

Self-regulation: Managing potential negative reactions like envy, competitiveness, or the urge to point out potential problems when your partner shares good news creates space for unalloyed celebration.

Empathy: Connecting emotionally with your partner's experience of joy or pride amplifies the positive impact for both of you.

Types of Celebration in Relationships

Celebration in relationships takes many forms, each serving important functions in building connection and positive emotion:

1. Achievement Celebrations

These acknowledge accomplishments, milestones, and goals reached—whether individual achievements (career advancement, personal goals) or relationship milestones (anniversaries, major purchases, relationship growth).

Why they matter: Achievement celebrations validate effort, mark progress, and create shared pride in each other's growth and in your journey together.

Example practices:

- Creating meaningful anniversary rituals that reflect on your journey and growth together
- Marking career achievements with special dinners or experiences
- Acknowledging personal growth milestones with thoughtful gifts or letters

2. Everyday Appreciation

These smaller, more frequent celebrations acknowledge the daily contributions, qualities, and moments that might otherwise go unnoticed.

Why they matter: Regular appreciation prevents the relationship from being taken for granted and helps partners feel seen and valued in their everyday efforts.

Example practices:

- Daily gratitude exchanges where you each share something you appreciated about the other

- "Appreciation ambushes"—unexpected notes or texts expressing specific appreciation

- Weekly reflection on "small wins" in your relationship or individual lives

3. Joy Rituals

These are intentional practices focused on creating and savoring positive experiences together.

Why they matter: Shared joy creates powerful bonding experiences and positive memories that strengthen your connection.

Example practices:

- Regular "play dates" where you engage in activities purely for enjoyment

- Savoring rituals where you intentionally prolong and enhance positive experiences

- Laughter practices like sharing humor, inside jokes, or playful interactions

4. Growth Acknowledgments

These celebrations recognize progress through challenges, learning from mistakes, and the courage to try difficult things—even when the outcome wasn't perfect.

Why they matter: Growth acknowledgments create safety for vulnerability and reinforce that effort and courage are valued alongside achievement.

Example practices:

- "Failure parties" that celebrate the learning from unsuccessful attempts

- Progress acknowledgments that mark improvement rather than just end results

- Courage recognitions that honor vulnerability and stepping outside comfort zones

Exercise: Celebration Styles Inventory
Time needed: 30-45 minutes **Materials**: Paper and pens
This exercise helps couples understand their unique celebration preferences:
Separately, each partner reflects on and writes about:
- How was celebration handled in your family of origin?

- What types of achievements or moments were celebrated, and how?

- What types of celebration make you feel most

appreciated and seen?

- What forms of celebration feel uncomfortable or inauthentic to you?

- What's one way you'd love to be celebrated that rarely or never happens?

Share your reflections with each other, asking curious questions to deepen understanding.

Together, create a "Celebration Preferences Guide" that captures:

- How each of you prefers to celebrate personal achievements

- How you'd like to mark relationship milestones

- What everyday appreciation looks like for each of you

- Any celebration approaches that feel uncomfortable and should be avoided

Use this guide to inform how you acknowledge and celebrate each other moving forward.

Exercise: The Good News Response Practice
Time needed: 5 minutes daily, as opportunities arise
Materials: None

Research by psychologist Shelly Gable identifies four ways partners typically respond when good news is shared:
- Active-Constructive: Enthusiastic, engaged response that asks for details and expresses genuine happiness (most relationship-enhancing)

- Passive-Constructive: Positive but minimal response without engagement

- Active-Destructive: Response that points out potential downsides or problems

- Passive-Destructive: Ignoring or changing the subject

This exercise helps couples practice the relationship-enhancing active-constructive response. When your partner shares good news (of any size), practice the active-constructive response:
- Show authentic enthusiasm (both verbally and non-verbally)

- Ask curious questions about the experience

- Help them savor by reflecting on what this means to them

- Express genuine happiness for them

- Notice the impact this response has on both your partner and your own emotional state.

At the end of each day, briefly reflect on opportunities you had to respond to good news and how you handled them.

Exercise: Relationship Wins Journal
Time needed: 15 minutes weekly **Materials**: Special journal or notebook, pens

This exercise creates a tangible record of positive relationship experiences:

- Choose a special journal dedicated solely to recording relationship "wins" of allsizes.

- Set a regular time (perhaps Sunday evening) to reflect together on the past week.

Take turns writing entries about:

- Moments of connection you experienced

- Challenges you navigated successfully together

- Things you appreciated about each other

- Progress you noticed in your relationship

- Joyful or meaningful experiences you shared

Periodically (perhaps monthly or on special occasions) review past entries together, savoring the accumulation of positive experiences.

During difficult times, use this journal as a resource to remind yourselves of your capacity for connection and joy together.

Exercise: Celebration Planning Workshop
Time needed: 60-90 minutes **Materials:** Calendar, paper and pens

This exercise helps couples be more intentional about building celebration into their relationship:
Together, identify upcoming opportunities for celebration in the next 3-6 months:
- Personal achievements or milestones

- Relationship anniversaries or milestones

- Seasonal events or holidays

- Completion of challenging projects or phases

For each opportunity, discuss:
- What would make this celebration meaningful for each of you?

- What preparation or planning is needed?

- How can you make this celebration reflect your unique relationship?

Schedule not just the celebrations themselves but also the planning time needed.

Create a "Spontaneous Celebration List" of ideas for unplanned moments of joy or achievement.

Commit to a balance of planned celebrations and spontaneous acknowledgments.

Overcoming Barriers to Celebration

Despite good intentions, many couples struggle to maintain a consistent celebration practice. Understanding common barriers can help you navigate these challenges:

Barrier 1: Busyness and Distraction

In our hyper-scheduled lives, celebration often gets crowded out by more "urgent" demands.

Solutions:

- Schedule celebration time with the same priority as other important commitments
- Create simple, brief celebration rituals that can fit into busy days
- Use technology intentionally (calendar reminders, apps) to prompt celebration
- Practice mindfulness to help you notice celebration-worthy moments amid busyness

Barrier 2: Celebration Discomfort

Some people feel uncomfortable with celebration due to family background, personality, or past experiences.

Solutions:

- Start with celebration forms that feel comfortable, gradually expanding your repertoire

- Discuss specific discomforts openly so your partner understands your reactions

- Create personalized celebration approaches that honor both partners' comfort levels

- Consider whether therapy might help address deeper celebration blocks

Barrier 3: Comparison and Perfectionism

The tendency to compare achievements to others' or to discount successes that aren't "perfect" can undermine celebration.

Solutions:

- Practice celebrating progress and effort, not just outcomes

- Establish a "no comparison" rule during celebration moments

- Create celebrations that focus on personal meaning rather than external metrics

- Challenge perfectionist thoughts that minimize achievements

Barrier 4: Celebration Inequality

When one partner's achievements or preferences consistently dominate celebration, resentment can develop.

Solutions:

- Track celebration focus to ensure balance over time
- Actively look for opportunities to celebrate the quieter partner's contributions
- Take turns planning celebrations to ensure both perspectives are represented
- Discuss any perceived imbalance openly and compassionately

Celebration Across the Relationship Lifecycle

How couples celebrate evolves across different relationship phases, each with unique opportunities and challenges:

New Relationships

Early relationships often have natural excitement and celebration as partners discover each other and experience many "firsts" together.

Focus areas:

- Establishing celebration rituals that can evolve with your relationship

- Noticing and appreciating each other's unique qualities

- Creating meaningful ways to mark relationship milestones

- Building a foundation of positive shared experiences

Established Relationships

Long-term relationships risk falling into celebration complacency as the novelty wears off and partners begin taking each other for granted.

Focus areas:

- Refreshing celebration approaches to prevent staleness

- Finding new aspects of your partner to appreciate and acknowledge

- Creating celebration rituals that evolve as your relationship matures

- Balancing familiar traditions with novel experiences

Relationships with Children

Parenting often shifts celebration focus to children, sometimes at the expense of the couple relationship.

Focus areas:

- Maintaining couple-centered celebrations alongside family celebrations

- Modeling healthy celebration for children by openly appreciating each other

- Finding ways to celebrate amid the constraints of parenting

- Including children in celebrating the relationship itself

Later-Life Relationships

As couples enter retirement or become empty-nesters, celebration opportunities and forms often shift significantly.

Focus areas:

- Celebrating the accumulated wisdom and history of your relationship

- Finding new shared interests to enjoy and celebrate together

- Acknowledging the transitions of aging with compassion and appreciation

- Creating legacy celebrations that connect to younger generations

Dialogue Scripts: Celebration in Conversation

Here are examples of language that enhances celebration in relationships:

When acknowledging achievements: "I'm so proud of how you handled that project. I know it stretched you in new ways, and I was impressed by how you navigated the challenges while staying true to your values."

When expressing daily appreciation: "I noticed how patient you were with the kids this morning when everyone was running late. That calm presence made such a difference in starting our day well."

When responding to good news: "That's wonderful! Tell me more about how it happened and how you're feeling about it. This is such a well-deserved recognition of your hard work."

When planning a celebration: "This milestone deserves special acknowledgment. What would feel most meaningful to you as a way to mark this achievement? I want to celebrate in a way that really resonates with what this means to you.

When acknowledging relationship growth: "I've been reflecting on how far we've come in how we communicate about difficult topics. Remember how those conversations used to go a year ago? I'm really proud of the work we've both put in to grow in this area."

Chapter Reflection: Your Celebration Journey

Take a moment to reflect on your current celebration practices:

1. What types of celebration come most naturally in your relationship? What types tend to be overlooked?

2. How do your celebration styles complement or challenge each other?

3. What's one achievement or quality in your partner that you haven't fully acknowledged recently?

4. What barriers most affect your ability to celebrate consistently?

5. What's one celebration practice from this chapter that you'd like to implement in the coming week?

The Bridge to the Next Chapter: From Celebration to Self-Growth

While celebration focuses on acknowledging what's already present in your relationship, continued growth requires intentional development—both individually and as a couple.

In the next chapter, we'll explore the role of self-growth in relationships, discovering how personal development enhances partnership and how the P.U.L.S.E. framework supports both individual and relational evolution.

We'll examine how to balance autonomy and togetherness, how to support each other's growth journeys, and how to ensure that individual development strengthens rather than threatens your connection.

But before we move on, I encourage you to begin implementing the celebration practices in this chapter. Remember that celebration, like any relationship skill, develops through consistent practice. Each time you pause to acknowledge, appreciate, and savor the positive in your relationship, you're not just creating a momentary good feeling—you're building a foundation of positivity that enhances your resilience, deepens your connection, and increases your capacity for joy together.

LOVE WITH P.U.L.S.E.

KEEP GOING AFTER THE CHAPTER ENDS

- Guided Video Exercises
- Printable Worksheets
- Real-Life Tools You Can Use Today

Turn what you just read into what you can actually do — right now.

Dr. Ashley R. Bryant
Creator of the P.U.L.S.E. Framework & Author of Love With P.U.L.S.E.

Already finished the book? Scan to access every chapter's bonus content in one place.

Chapter 12
The Role of Self-Growth in Relationships

A thriving relationship is not just about how two people interact with each other—it's also about how each person continues to develop as an individual. The healthiest partnerships are those where both people maintain their unique identities and pursue personal growth while simultaneously nurturing their connection. This balance between autonomy and togetherness creates relationships that are both secure and dynamic, providing both roots and wings.

In this chapter, we'll explore the vital role of self-growth in relationship success, how to support each other's individual journeys, and how the P.U.L.S.E. framework can help you create a partnership that encourages both personal development and deeper connection. We'll discover that far from being selfish, appropriate self-focus actually enhances your capacity for genuine intimacy and lasting love.

The Paradox of Self-Growth in Relationships

Many people enter relationships with an unconscious belief that true love means merging identities—sacrificing individual needs, interests, and growth for the sake of the partnership. This belief, while romantic-sounding, actually undermines relationship health over time. When partners lose their individual identities, the relationship itself suffers from stagnation, resentment, and diminished attraction.

The paradox is this: maintaining appropriate separateness and individual development actually creates the conditions for deeper connection. When both partners continue to grow, learn, and evolve as individuals, they bring fresh energy, perspectives, and capacities to their relationship. They remain interesting to each other. They have more to share. And perhaps most importantly, they choose the relationship freely rather than from dependency or obligation.

Case Study: The Growth Imbalance

When Sophia and Marcus married in their early twenties, they were at similar stages of personal development. Over the next decade, Sophia pursued ongoing education, developed new interests, built a diverse social network, and regularly challenged herself to step outside her comfort zone. Marcus, meanwhile, settled into comfortable routines, stopped pursuing new interests, and primarily socialized with the same small group they'd known since college.

By their mid-thirties, they found themselves struggling with a growing sense of disconnection. Sophia felt Marcus couldn't relate to important parts of her evolving identity and interests. Marcus felt increasingly inadequate and threatened by Sophia's growth, responding with subtle criticism of her new pursuits and friends.

Through couples therapy, they recognized this growth imbalance was at the heart of their disconnection. Marcus realized his stagnation stemmed partly from fear—of failure, of change, of potentially growing apart. With Sophia's support, he began exploring new interests and challenging himself again. Sophia learned to better include Marcus in her growth journey, sharing her experiences in ways that invited connection rather than highlighting their differences.

As Marcus reconnected with his own development path, their relationship regained its vitality. They discovered that supporting each other's growth actually brought them closer, creating new shared experiences and deeper appreciation for each other's unique qualities and journeys.

The P.U.L.S.E. Approach to Self-Growth in Relationships

The five elements of the P.U.L.S.E. framework provide powerful tools for supporting both individual development and relationship connection:

Praise: Acknowledging and celebrating your partner's growth efforts and achievements creates safety for continued development. "I admire how you've been challenging yourself with that new project—your creativity and persistence are really inspiring."

Understanding: Making the effort to comprehend your partner's growth aspirations and the values behind them, even when they differ from your own priorities.

Listening: Creating space for your partner to process their personal journey, including struggles and breakthroughs, without immediately relating it back to yourself or the relationship.

Self-regulation: Managing potential feelings of insecurity, jealousy, or abandonment that can arise when your partner pursues independent growth, allowing you to respond supportively rather than restrictively.

Empathy: Connecting with your partner's emotional experience of their growth journey—the excitement, fears, frustrations, and triumphs—even when their path is different from yours.

Balancing Autonomy and Connection: The Growth-Together Spectrum

Healthy relationships exist on a spectrum between complete autonomy (living essentially parallel lives) and complete togetherness (merged identity with little individual space).

Neither extreme supports optimal relationship health or personal development.

The ideal balance—what we might call "growth-together"—involves:

Secure Attachment: A strong emotional bond that provides safety and support for individual exploration.

Differentiation: The ability to maintain a clear sense of self while in close relationship, neither becoming enmeshed nor emotionally cut off.

Mutual Support: Active encouragement of each other's growth and development, even when it temporarily takes time or focus away from the relationship.

Shared Meaning: Connecting individual growth journeys to shared values and relationship vision.

Flexible Togetherness: Moving fluidly between periods of individual focus and deep connection, without anxiety or resentment.

> **Exercise: Mapping Your Growth-Together Balance**
> **Time needed**: 45-60 minutes **Materials**: Paper and pens, optional colored markers
> This exercise helps couples assess and enhance their current autonomy-connection balance:
> Draw a horizontal line across a sheet of paper. Label the left end "Complete Autonomy" and the right end "Complete Togetherness."

Separately, each partner marks where they believe your relationship currently falls on this spectrum. Also mark where you personally would feel most fulfilled.

Share your markings and discuss:
- Are there differences in how you perceive your current balance?
- Are there differences in your ideal points on the spectrum?
- What factors might influence these perceptions and preferences?

Together, identify specific areas of your relationship where you might benefit from:
- More autonomy and individual space
- More connection and togetherness
- Better integration of individual pursuits into your shared life

Create a concrete plan for adjusting your balance in these areas over the next month.

Supporting Your Partner's Growth Journey

One of the greatest gifts you can offer your partner is genuine support for their personal development. This support goes beyond simple permission or passive acceptance—it involves active encouragement, practical assistance, and emotional backing for their growth pursuits.

LOVE WITH P.U.L.S.E.

KEEP GOING AFTER THE CHAPTER ENDS

- Guided Video Exercises
- Printable Worksheets
- Real-Life Tools You Can Use Today

Turn what you just read into what you can actually do — right now.

Dr. Ashley R. Bryant

Creator of the P.U.L.S.E. Framework & Author of Love With P.U.L.S.E.

Already finished the book? Scan to access every chapter's bonus content in one place.

CHAPTER 13
Supporting Mental and Emotional Well-Being

In our journey through the P.U.L.S.E. framework, we've explored how to build connection, navigate conflict, celebrate successes, and support individual growth.

Underlying all these aspects of a thriving relationship is perhaps the most fundamental foundation: mental and emotional well-being. When partners nurture both their own psychological health and create a relationship environment that supports emotional wellness, they build capacity for all other dimensions of connection.

In this chapter, we'll explore how couples can support each other's mental and emotional well-being while maintaining appropriate boundaries and self-care. We'll discover how the P.U.L.S.E. framework provides powerful tools for navigating mental health challenges, creating emotionally nurturing environments, and building relationships that enhance rather than drain each partner's psychological resources.

The Relationship-Wellbeing Connection

The connection between relationship quality and mental health flows in both directions:

Relationship Impact on Mental Health: Research consistently shows that relationship satisfaction is one of the strongest predictors of overall life satisfaction and mental wellbeing. Supportive partnerships buffer against stress, reduce risk for depression and anxiety, and even strengthen immune function. Conversely, relationship distress is linked to increased mental health symptoms and reduced physical health.

Mental Health Impact on Relationships: Individual psychological wellbeing significantly affects relationship functioning. When one or both partners struggle with mental health challenges, relationships often face increased stress, communication difficulties, and intimacy barriers. This bidirectional influence creates both challenge and opportunity. The challenge lies in preventing relationship difficulties and mental health issues from creating negative spirals. The opportunity lies in harnessing the power of your relationship as a healing force while simultaneously using mental health practices to strengthen your connection.

Case Study: Breaking the Negative Spiral

When Jamie began experiencing symptoms of anxiety and depression following a job loss, the impact quickly rippled through their relationship with Alex. Jamie withdrew emotionally, had little energy for shared activities, and became irritable over small frustrations. Alex, unsure how to help, alternated between walking on eggshells and pushing Jamie to "snap out of it"—approaches that inadvertently increased Jamie's stress and feelings of inadequacy.

As Jamie's symptoms worsened, the relationship tension escalated, creating a negative feedback loop where relationship stress exacerbated mental health symptoms, which further strained the relationship. This pattern continued until Alex reached out to a couples therapist who specialized in relationships affected by mental health challenges.

Through therapy, they learned to break this cycle. Jamie began appropriate individual treatment while also learning to communicate more clearly about their experience and needs. Alex developed better understanding of anxiety and depression and learned supportive responses that helped rather than hindered Jamie's recovery. They created relationship practices that accommodated Jamie's current limitations while maintaining essential connection.

Over time, this approach transformed their negative spiral into a positive one: as the relationship became more supportive, Jamie's symptoms improved, which further enhanced their connection. While recovery wasn't linear, they developed a shared understanding that allowed them to navigate fluctuations in Jamie's mental health without the relationship deteriorating.

The P.U.L.S.E. Approach to Emotional Wellbeing

The five elements of the P.U.L.S.E. framework provide powerful tools for supporting mental and emotional health in relationships:

Praise: Acknowledging and appreciating efforts toward mental health, however small, reinforces positive steps and builds confidence. "I noticed you used that breathing technique when you felt anxious earlier—I really admire your commitment to developing those skills."

Understanding: Making the effort to comprehend mental health challenges—both through general education and specific learning about your partner's unique experience—creates a foundation for effective support.

Listening: Creating space for your partner to express their emotional experience without judgment, minimization, or immediate problem-solving allows for the healing power of being truly heard.

Self-regulation: Managing your own emotional reactions to your partner's mental health challenges—whether frustration, helplessness, or anxiety—enables you to remain a steady, supportive presence.

Empathy: Connecting with your partner's emotional experience, even when it differs from your own or seems disproportionate to the situation, validates their reality and reduces isolation.

Creating an Emotionally Safe Relationship Environment

One of the most powerful ways partners can support each other's mental health is by creating a relationship environment where all emotions are welcomed, validated, and responded to with care. This emotional safety becomes particularly crucial during mental health challenges, when emotions may be more intense or volatile.

Key Elements of Emotional Safety:

Emotion Validation: Acknowledging the legitimacy of all feelings without judgment or minimization. "It makes sense that you'd feel that way, given your experience."

Permission for the Full Emotional Spectrum: Creating space for the expression of difficult emotions like anger, fear, or sadness without punishment or withdrawal.

Emotional Attunement: Noticing subtle cues about your partner's emotional state and responding with appropriate care.

Repair After Emotional Injuries: Quickly addressing moments where emotional safety was compromised through sincere apology and changed behavior.

Predictable Emotional Responses: Developing consistent, supportive reactions to vulnerability that build trust over time.

Exercise: Emotional Safety Assessment and Enhancement

Time needed: 45-60 minutes **Materials**: Paper and pens

This exercise helps couples evaluate and improve their emotional safety:

Separately, each partner reflects on and writes about:

- When do you feel most emotionally safe in our relationship?

- When do you feel least emotionally safe?

- What specific behaviors help you feel your emotions are welcomed and validated?

- What responses make you want to hide or suppress your feelings?

- What's one thing your partner could do to help you feel more emotionally safe?

Share your reflections with each other, listening with openness and without defensiveness.

Together, create an "Emotional Safety Agreement" that includes:

- Specific behaviors you each commit to when the other shares difficult emotions

- Phrases or approaches to avoid during emotional vulnerability

- How you'll signal when you're feeling emotionally

unsafe

- How you'll repair moments when emotional safety is compromised

Practice implementing this agreement, with regular check-ins to refine your approach based on experience.

Supporting a Partner Through Mental Health Challenges

When your partner experiences mental health difficulties—whether temporary struggles like grief or adjustment stress, or more persistent conditions like anxiety, depression, or trauma responses—your support can significantly impact both their wellbeing and your relationship quality. Effective support requires balancing compassion with appropriate boundaries.

Practical Support Strategies:

Educate Yourself: Learn about your partner's specific mental health challenges through reputable sources, while recognizing that their individual experience may differ from general descriptions.

Separate Person from Problem: Practice seeing your partner as distinct from their mental health condition—they are not their anxiety, depression, or other challenges.

Validate Without Reinforcing: Acknowledge the reality of their experience without inadvertently reinforcing unhelpful patterns. "I can see you're feeling really anxious right now, and that's really hard" rather than "You're right, that situation is terrifying."

Encourage Treatment While Respecting Autonomy: Support professional help seeking without forcing or controlling the process. "I'm here to support you in finding help that works for you" rather than "You need to see a therapist immediately."

Maintain Relationship Dimensions Beyond Mental Health: Continue to connect around other aspects of life and your relationship, preventing mental health challenges from becoming the relationship's sole focus.

Practice Compassionate Accountability: Support your partner in taking responsibility for their mental health and its impact on the relationship, while acknowledging the real limitations their challenges may create.

Exercise: Support Planning for Mental Health Challenges

Time needed: 60 minutes **Materials**: Paper and pens
This exercise helps couples develop specific support strategies for mental health difficulties:
Together, identify specific mental health challenges that affect your relationship (e.g., anxiety episodes, depressive periods, trauma triggers).

For each challenge, discuss:
- What are the early warning signs that this challenge is emerging?
- What typically helps when this challenge is present?
- What responses tend to make things worse?
- What specific support would be most helpful from the partner?
- What self-care is needed by the supporting partner during these times?

Create a concrete support plan for each identified challenge, including:
- Specific supportive actions and phrases
- Approaches or comments to avoid
- When and how to encourage professional support
- How to maintain connection during difficult periods
- How to care for the relationship while navigating the challenge

Schedule regular reviews of these plans, updating them based on experience and changing circumstances.

Self-Care While Supporting a Partner

Supporting a partner through mental health challenges can be emotionally demanding.Without appropriate self-care, partners risk compassion fatigue, resentment, or evensecondary trauma. Maintaining your own wellbeing isn't selfish—it's essential forsustainable support and relationship health.

Essential Self-Care Practices:

Maintain Your Own Support System: Cultivate relationships and resources outside your partnership where you can process your experiences and receive emotional support.

Set Appropriate Boundaries: Clarify what support you can realistically provide and what might require professional help or additional resources.

Practice Emotional Differentiation: Develop the capacity to empathize with your partner's distress without absorbing it as your own or feeling responsible for fixing it.

Preserve Personal Renewal Activities: Continue practices that replenish your emotional and physical energy, even when your partner's needs seem pressing.

Consider Support Groups or Therapy: Specialized resources for partners of those with mental health challenges can provide validation, education, and coping strategies.

Exercise: Self-Care Assessment and Planning

Time needed: 30-45 minutes **Materials:** Journal or paper, pen

This exercise helps supporting partners develop sustainable self-care:

Reflect on and write about:
- How has supporting your partner's mental health affected your own wellbeing?

- What signs indicate that you might be approaching compassion fatigue or burnout?

- What activities or practices reliably replenish your emotional resources?

- What boundaries might you need to establish or strengthen?

- What additional support would help you maintain your own wellbeing?

Create a specific self-care plan that includes:
- Daily practices for emotional and physical wellbeing

- Weekly activities that provide deeper renewal

- Clear boundaries around your support capacity

- Specific outside resources you'll utilize

- How you'll communicate your needs to your partner

Share appropriate parts of this plan with your partner, focusing on how your self-care ultimately benefits both of you and the relationship.mImplement your plan consistently, adjusting as needed based on experience.

Navigating Specific Mental Health Challenges in Relationships

While general principles apply broadly, certain mental health challenges present unique relationship dynamics that benefit from specific approaches:

Anxiety Disorders

Anxiety can lead to reassurance-seeking, avoidance behaviors, and difficulty with uncertainty—all of which can create relationship patterns that inadvertently reinforce anxiety.

Helpful Approaches:

- Avoid providing excessive reassurance that reinforces anxiety cycles

- Support gradual exposure to anxiety, provoking situations rather than enabling avoidance

- Develop clear agreements about how to respond during anxiety episodes

- Recognize and interrupt accommodation patterns

that maintain anxiety

Depression

Depression often manifests as withdrawal, reduced interest in shared activities, irritability, and negative thinking patterns that can strain relationship connection.

Helpful Approaches:

- Balance compassion for genuine limitations with gentle encouragement toward activities that might improve mood
- Maintain connection through simplified interactions when energy is low
- Challenge the depression narrative ("You don't care about me") rather than the depressed person
- Create a depression action plan during better periods to implement during difficult times

Trauma Responses

Past trauma can impact relationships through triggers, emotional regulation difficulties, trust issues, and intimacy challenges.

Helpful Approaches:

- Develop awareness of potential triggers and

collaborative strategies for managing them

- Create safety plans for triggered states that respect both partners' needs

- Recognize that trauma responses aren't personal or intentional

- Support trauma-informed therapy while avoiding taking on a therapist role

Substance Use Concerns

Substance use issues create unique relationship challenges including trust erosion, inconsistent behavior, and enabling dynamics.

Helpful Approaches:

- Establish clear boundaries that protect your wellbeing while supporting recovery

- Avoid both enabling and controlling behaviors

- Seek specialized support for yourself regardless of your partner's recovery choices

- Recognize the importance of your partner's internal motivation for lasting change

When Professional Support Is Needed

While relationship support is valuable for mental health, it's important to recognize when professional help is needed. Partners can play a crucial role in encouraging appropriate treatment while respecting autonomy in the process.

Signs Professional Support May Be Beneficial:

- Symptoms significantly impact daily functioning for more than two weeks

- Self-harm thoughts or behaviors are present

- Substance use is interfering with health, relationships, or responsibilities

- Relationship patterns are consistently reinforcing mental health difficulties

- Supporting partner is experiencing significant distress or compassion fatigue

- Basic support strategies aren't creating improvement over time

Approaches to Encouraging Professional Help:

Express Care Rather Than Criticism: "I'm concerned about how much you're suffering" rather than "You need to get help because your anxiety is ruining our relationship."

Offer Practical Assistance: "Would it help if I researched some therapists or sat with you while you make the call?" rather than "You need to find a therapist."

Share Observed Impact: "I've noticed you haven't been able to enjoy things you usually love" rather than "You're always negative lately."

Consider Relationship Therapy First: Sometimes starting with couples therapy feels less threatening and can serve as a bridge to individual treatment when needed.

Respect Readiness: Recognize that forcing treatment rarely works; supporting readiness through compassionate, consistent conversations is more effective.

Dialogue Example: Encouraging Professional Support

Partner A: "I've noticed you've been having trouble sleeping and seem to be worrying a lot more than usual. It seems like it's really wearing on you."

Partner B: "I'm fine. Everyone gets stressed sometimes."

Partner A: "You're right that everyone experiences stress. I'm just concerned because this seems different from your usual stress—it's been going on for a while now and seems to be affecting you more deeply. I care about you and hate seeing you struggle so much."

Partner B: "I don't think it's that bad. What would I even say to a therapist?"

Partner A: "You'd just share what you're experiencing, similar to what you've shared with me. I found it really helpful when I talked to someone during my difficult time last year.

Would it help if I shared what that process was like for me? Or maybe we could look at some options together?"

Partner B: "I'll think about it. Maybe you could tell me more about how it worked for you."

This dialogue demonstrates expressing concern without judgment, normalizing professional support, offering practical assistance, and respecting the partner's pace in considering help.

Building Daily Mental Wellness Practices as a Couple

Beyond addressing specific mental health challenges, couples can proactively build relationship practices that enhance emotional wellbeing for both partners. These shared wellness routines create a foundation of psychological health that strengthens resilience and deepens connection.

Couple Wellness Practices:

Emotional Check-Ins: Brief, regular opportunities to share current emotional states without problem-solving. "On a scale of 1-10, how's your emotional weather today? What's contributing to that?"

Stress-Reduction Rituals: Shared practices that calm the nervous system, such as breathing exercises, meditation, or gentle movement.

Nature Connection: Regular time outdoors together, which research shows significantly benefits mental health.

Gratitude Practices: Routines that direct attention to positive aspects of life and the relationship, counterbalancing negativity bias.

Sleep Hygiene Collaboration: Supporting each other's healthy sleep habits, recognizing sleep's crucial role in emotional regulation.

Digital Wellness: Shared agreements about technology use that protect mental space and relationship connection.

Exercise: Creating Your Couple Wellness Plan
Time needed: 45-60 minutes **Materials**: Paper and pens, calendar
This exercise helps couples develop sustainable mental wellness practices:
Together, discuss which aspects of mental wellness feel most important to each of you right now:
- Stress management

- Mood regulation

- Anxiety reduction

- Present-moment awareness

- Emotional connection

- Physical wellbeing that supports mental health

For each priority area, brainstorm practices you might implement together:
- Daily micro-practices (5 minutes or less)

- Weekly longer practices (15-30 minutes)

- Monthly deeper experiences (1-3 hours)

Select 2-3 practices to implement immediately, considering:
- Mutual interest and motivation

- Realistic fit with your current lifestyle

- Potential impact on your specific wellness needs

Create specific implementation plans for each selected practice:
- When and where will it happen?

- What resources or preparation are needed?

- How will you remind each other and maintain

accountability?

- How will you evaluate whether it's helping?

Schedule a one-month review to assess how these practices are working and make adjustments as needed.

Dialogue Scripts: Supporting Emotional Wellbeing in Conversation

Here are examples of communication that fosters mental and emotional health in relationships:

When checking in about emotional state: "How's your heart today? I'd really like to understand what's going on for you emotionally, without trying to fix anything—just to be with you in whatever you're experiencing."

When noticing potential mental health concerns: "I've noticed some changes in your patterns lately, like having trouble sleeping and seeming more withdrawn. I'm wondering how you're feeling and if there's anything you'd like to share about what's going on for you."

When offering support during difficult emotions: "It seems like you're having a really hard time right now. I'm here with you in this. Would it help to talk about it, or would you prefer some quiet support right now? I'm open to whatever would feel most helpful."

When setting a boundary while still being supportive: "I care deeply about supporting you through this difficult time. I'm noticing I'm feeling depleted myself and need to recharge a bit. Could we figure out a way for me to take a short break while making sure you still have the support you need?"

When acknowledging improvement: "I've noticed you seem to have more energy lately and have been more engaged in activities you enjoy. I'm really happy to see that and wonder what you think might be contributing to that positive shift?"

Chapter Reflection: Your Emotional Wellbeing Journey

Take a moment to reflect on mental and emotional wellbeing in your relationship:

1. How effectively does your relationship currently support each partner's emotional health? What's working well, and what could be improved?

2. What specific mental health challenges affect your relationship, either consistently or periodically? How might you better navigate these together?

3. What boundaries around mental health support might need clarification or adjustment in your relationship?

4. What wellness practices could you implement or strengthen to enhance both individual and

relationship emotional health?

5. How might you use the P.U.L.S.E. framework more effectively to create a relationship environment that nurtures psychological wellbeing?

The Bridge to the Next Chapter: From Emotional Wellbeing to StressManagement

While this chapter has focused broadly on mental and emotional health, one specific challenge deserves particular attention: stress. In the next chapter, we'll explore how couples can effectively manage stress together, preventing it from eroding their connection while using it as an opportunity to strengthen their bond. We'll discover how the P.U.L.S.E. framework provides specific tools for navigating both everyday stressors and major life challenges, transforming potential relationship threats into opportunities for deeper support and connection. But before we move on, I encourage you to begin implementing the emotional wellbeing practices in this chapter. Remember that mental health in relationships isn't about perfection—it's about creating an environment where both partners feel safe to be authentic, receive appropriate support, and grow through both challenges and joys. Each step you take toward greater emotional safety and wellbeing builds your capacity for the deep, lasting connection that makes relationships truly fulfilling.

LOVE WITH P.U.L.S.E.

KEEP GOING AFTER THE CHAPTER ENDS

- Guided Video Exercises
- Printable Worksheets
- Real-Life Tools You Can Use Today

Turn what you just read into what you can actually do — right now.

Dr. Ashley R. Bryant

Creator of the P.U.L.S.E. Framework & Author of Love With P.U.L.S.E.

Already finished the book? Scan to access every chapter's bonus content in one place.

CHAPTER 14
Managing Stress Together

In today's fast-paced world, stress has become an inevitable part of life. From work pressures and financial concerns to family responsibilities and health challenges, stressors constantly compete for our attention and energy. While we often think of stress as an individual experience, its impact on relationships is profound. How couples navigate stress—both shared challenges and individual pressures—can either strengthen their bond or create distance and conflict.

In this chapter, we'll explore how to effectively manage stress as a team, transforming potential relationship threats into opportunities for deeper connection and support. We'll discover how the P.U.L.S.E. framework provides specific tools for navigating both everyday stressors and major life challenges, helping you build a relationship that thrives even under pressure.

Understanding Stress in Relationships

Stress affects relationships in two primary ways:

- Stress Spillover: When stress from outside sources

(work, finances, health) "spills over" into the relationship, affecting how partners interact with each other. This often manifests as increased irritability, decreased patience, reduced emotional availability, or withdrawal.

- Stress Generation: When the relationship itself becomes a source of stress through conflict, misunderstanding, or unmet needs. This creates a particularly challenging dynamic as the relationship simultaneously becomes both a source of stress and the context in which that stress must be managed.

Research shows that couples who develop effective stress management strategies experience greater relationship satisfaction, better communication during difficult times, and increased resilience to life's inevitable challenges.

Case Study: The Stress Cycle

Miguel and Sophia had always prided themselves on their strong relationship. But when Miguel took on a demanding new role at work with longer hours and higher pressure, their connection began to fray. Exhausted and mentally drained at the end of each day, Miguel had little energy for meaningful conversation or shared activities. Sophia, feeling increasingly disconnected, began to interpret Miguel's withdrawal as lack of interest in the relationship.

As Sophia expressed her dissatisfaction, Miguel felt criticized and misunderstood—didn't she see how hard he was working? This created additional relationship tension, which further depleted Miguel's coping resources and made him even less emotionally available. Sophia, in turn, felt more abandoned and frustrated, creating a negative cycle that neither knew how to break.

Through couples counseling, they learned to recognize this pattern as a stress cycle rather than a relationship problem at its core. They developed strategies to support Miguel's stress management while maintaining essential connection points in their relationship. Most importantly, they learned to view stress as a shared challenge to navigate together rather than an individual burden or relationship threat.

The P.U.L.S.E. Approach to Stress Management

The five elements of the P.U.L.S.E. framework provide powerful tools for managing stress as a couple:

Praise: Acknowledging and appreciating each other's efforts during stressful periods builds resilience and prevents stress from being interpreted as relationship disinterest. "I see how hard you're working to handle this situation while still making time for us."

Understanding: Making the effort to comprehend your partner's unique stress responses and needs creates the foundation for effective support. Different people experience and process stress differently, and what helps one person might not help another.

Listening: Creating space for your partner to express their stress-related thoughts and feelings without judgment or immediate problem-solving allows for emotional processing that reduces stress's impact.

Self-regulation: Managing your own stress responses prevents escalation during tense moments and allows you to remain a source of support rather than additional stress for your partner.

Empathy: Connecting with your partner's emotional experience of stress, even when you might not find the same situation stressful, validates their reality and strengthens your bond during challenging times.

Recognizing Stress Patterns in Your Relationship

Before you can effectively manage stress together, you need to understand how stress typically manifests in your specific relationship. Most couples develop characteristic patterns in how they respond to and interact around stress.

Common Stress Response Patterns:

Pursuer-Distancer: One partner seeks connection and communication when stressed (pursuer), while the other needs space and solitude to process (distancer). This natural difference can create a painful cycle where the pursuer's attempts at connection increase the distancer's need for space, and the distancer's withdrawal intensifies the pursuer's anxiety and pursuit.

Co-Escalation: Both partners become increasingly activated under stress, leading to heightened emotional reactivity and potential conflict. Each partner's stress response amplifies the other's, creating a spiral of escalating tension.

Mutual Withdrawal: Both partners retreat into themselves when stressed, creating emotional distance and lack of support when it's most needed. The relationship may feel like it's "on hold" until the stressful period passes.

Caretaker-Receiver: One partner consistently takes on the role of supporting the other through stress, potentially creating imbalance and caretaker burnout over time if the pattern isn't reciprocal.

Problem-Solver vs. Emotion-Processor: One partner approaches stress by focusing on practical solutions, while the other needs emotional processing before considering solutions. This difference can create frustration when each partner offers the type of support they would want rather than what their partner needs.

Exercise: Mapping Your Stress Patterns

Time needed: 45-60 minutes Materials: Paper and pens
This exercise helps couples identify their characteristic stress patterns:
Separately, each partner reflects on and writes about:

- How do you typically know you're stressed? What are your physical, emotional, and behavioral indicators?

- What do you most need from your partner when you're stressed?

- What tends to increase your stress in relationship interactions?

- What helps you feel supported and understood during stressful times?

- How might your stress responses impact your partner?

Share your reflections with each other, asking clarifying questions to deepen understanding.

Together, identify your typical stress interaction patterns:

- Do you tend toward pursuer-distancer dynamics, co-escalation, mutual withdrawal, or another pattern?

- How do your individual stress responses interact with each other?

- What cycles or patterns have you noticed in how stress affects your relationship?

Create a "Stress Pattern Map" that visually represents how stress typically flows through your relationship, noting trigger points, escalation patterns, and potential intervention points.

Discuss how awareness of these patterns might help you interrupt unhelpful cycles and support each other more effectively during future stressful periods.

Building Your Stress Management Toolkit

Once you understand your stress patterns, you can develop specific strategies for managing stress both individually and as a couple. The most effective approach combines personal stress management practices with relationship-focused strategies.

Individual Stress Management Practices:

Physiological Regulation: Techniques that calm the body's stress response system, such as deep breathing, progressive muscle relaxation, or physical exercise.

Cognitive Strategies: Approaches that address stress-inducing thought patterns, such as perspective-taking, challenging catastrophic thinking, or mindfulness practices.

Emotional Processing: Methods for acknowledging and working through difficult emotions, such as journaling, creative expression, or talking with supportive others.

Boundary Setting: Practices that protect your energy and resources, such as saying no to additional commitments or limiting exposure to stressful situations when possible.

Renewal Activities: Experiences that replenish your emotional and physical resources, such as time in nature, engaging in hobbies, or connecting with supportive friends.

Relationship-Focused Stress Strategies:

Stress Communication Protocol: Agreed-upon approaches for sharing when you're experiencing stress and what support would be helpful.

Support Matching: Providing the specific type of support your partner needs rather than what you would want in their situation.

Stress Buffering: Creating relationship experiences that counterbalance life stressors, such as humor, physical affection, or shared enjoyable activities.

Division of Labor: Temporarily adjusting responsibilities when one partner is experiencing high stress to prevent overwhelm.

Stress-Specific Check-ins: Brief, regular conversations focused specifically on current stressors and support needs.

Exercise: Creating Your Couple Stress Management Plan
Time needed: 60 minutes Materials: Paper and pens

This exercise helps couples develop a comprehensive approach to managing stress together:

Individual Stress Management:
- Each partner identifies 3-5 personal stress management practices they commit to implementing regularly
- Discuss how you can support each other in maintaining these individual practices
- Create accountability structures that work for your relationship style

Early Warning System:
- Identify specific indicators that stress is beginning to affect your relationship
- Create agreements about how you'll signal to each other when you notice these warning signs
- Develop a plan for early intervention before stress patterns escalate

Support Strategies:
- For each partner, create a specific "stress support menu" listing helpful and unhelpful responses
- Include concrete examples of what supportive statements, actions, and presence look like
- Discuss how support needs might differ depending on the type or intensity of stress

Connection Preservation:
- Identify relationship connection points you commit to maintaining even during high-stress periods
- Create simple rituals that help you reconnect when stress has created distance
- Discuss how you'll protect your relationship from being completely overshadowed by external stressors

Implementation Plan:
- Schedule a regular "stress check-in" to review how your management strategies are working
- Create reminders or visual cues for your agreed-upon approaches
- Discuss how you'll compassionately redirect if you notice old patterns emerging

Navigating Specific Stressors Together

While general stress management principles apply broadly, certain common stressors benefit from specific approaches:

Work Stress

Work-related stress is among the most common external pressures affecting relationships, particularly when work demands conflict with relationship needs.

Helpful Approaches:

- Create clear boundaries between work and relationship time, perhaps through transition rituals
- Develop specific communication about when work needs must temporarily take priority
- Balance periods of intense work focus with intentional relationship reconnection
- Support career decisions that might reduce stress, even if they involve financial adjustments

Financial Stress

Money concerns consistently rank among the top relationship stressors, combining practical pressures with emotional and value-based dimensions.

Helpful Approaches:

- Separate practical financial discussions from emotional processing about money stress
- Create a structured approach to financial conversations that feels safe for both partners
- Acknowledge different money histories and how they

affect current stress responses

- Focus on shared financial values and goals rather that just numbers and budgets

Family and Parenting Stress

The demands of parenting and extended family relationships create unique stressors that directly impact couple dynamics.

Helpful Approaches:

- Maintain regular couple time that isn't focused on parenting or family issues

- Present a united front with children and extended family while processing differences privately

- Create explicit agreements about division of family responsibilities, especially during high-stress periods

- Recognize and address whenfamily patterns from your upbringing are affecting current stress responses

Health-Related Stress

Health challenges—whether acute or chronic, physical or mental—create significant relationship stress through practical demands, emotional impact, and role changes.

Helpful Approaches:

- Distinguish between the person and the health condition to prevent the relationship from being defined by illness

- Balance caretaking responsibilities with maintaining aspects of your romantic/partnership relationship

- Create regular opportunities to check in about how health challenges are affecting both partners

- Utilize outside support resources to prevent caregiver burnout and relationship strain

Major Life Transitions

Significant changes like moves, career shifts, or family structure changes create stress even when the changes are positive.

Helpful Approaches:

- Acknowledge that transitions affect each partner differently and at different paces

- Create rituals to mark endings and beginnings during major changes

- Maintain some stability elements (relationship rituals, familiar objects) during periods of change

- Regularly check in about adjustment processes

without judgment about different adaptation timelines

Stress-Proofing Your Relationship: Preventative Practices

Beyond responding to stress when it occurs, couples can implement regular practices that build their stress resilience before challenges arise. These preventative approaches create a relationship foundation that can withstand pressure without cracking.

Daily Practices (5-15 minutes):

Emotional Temperature Checks: Brief check-ins about current stress levels and support needs. "On a scale of 1-10, how's your stress today? Is there anything you need from me?"

Appreciation Exchanges: Sharing specific gratitude for how your partner has supported you or managed their responsibilities despite stress.

Physical Connection: Brief but intentional physical touch that releases oxytocin and counteracts stress hormones—a six-second hug, hand-holding during conversation, or a genuine kiss goodbye and hello.

Transition Rituals: Brief practices that help you shift from individual stress to couple connection, such as a few minutes of deep breathing together or sharing a highlight from your day before dinner.

Weekly Practices (30-60 minutes):

Stress Check-in Conversations: Structured time to discuss current stressors, support needs, and stress management successes.

Shared Relaxation: Activities that calm both partners' nervous systems, such as walking in nature, gentle stretching together, or shared meditation.

Proactive Problem-Solving: Addressing potential stressors before they become crises, perhaps through weekly planning or resource management discussions.

Joy Scheduling: Planning and protecting time for activities that bring mutual enjoyment and counterbalance life stressors.

Monthly Practices (1-3 hours):

Relationship Reflection: Deeper conversations about how you're navigating stress together, what's working well, and what adjustments might help.

Stress Pattern Reviews: Checking whether old stress response patterns have been reemerging and how you might interrupt them more effectively.

Resource Assessment: Evaluating whether your current resources (time, energy, support, finances) align with your commitments and making adjustments as needed.

Celebration and Acknowledgment: Recognizing how you've successfully navigated stressors together and what you've learned through the process.

Exercise: Stress-Proofing Implementation Plan
Time needed: 30-45 minutes Materials: Calendar, paper and pens
This exercise helps couples implement preventative stress-management practices:
Review the daily, weekly, and monthly practices above and identify which seem most relevant to your specific relationship needs.
For each timeframe (daily, weekly, monthly), select 1-2 practices to implement consistently.
For each selected practice:

- Discuss what specifically this would look like in your relationship

- Identify potential barriers to consistent implementation

- Create specific plans for when, where, and how you'll engage in this practice

- Determine how you'll remind each other and maintain accountability

Schedule these practices in your shared calendar or create another visible reminder system.

Commit to a three-month trial period, after which you'll evaluate what's working well and what needs adjustment.

Supporting Your Partner During Acute Stress

While ongoing stress management practices build general resilience, acute stress situations—like job loss, family emergencies, or health crises—require specific support approaches. During these high-stress periods, partners need to adjust their expectations and support strategies to match the intensity of the situation.

Effective Acute Stress Support:

Presence Before Solutions: During acute stress, emotional presence often matters more than practical help. Simply being with your partner in their distress—without trying to fix, minimize, or rush through the emotions—provides crucial support.

Practical Relief: Taking on additional responsibilities temporarily to create space for your partner to process and recover from acute stress.

Permission for Imperfection: Explicitly communicating that during high-stress periods, normal expectations around communication, household management, or relationship maintenance can be temporarily adjusted.

Buffering: Protecting your stressed partner from additional demands or stressors when possible, such as filtering non-urgent information or managing extended family communications during a crisis.

Recalibrated Connection: Finding simplified ways to maintain essential connection during acute stress periods, recognizing that elaborate date nights or deep conversations might not be feasible.

Dialogue Example: Supporting During Acute Stress

Partner A: "I know you just got that difficult news about your mom's health. I'm here for you. Do you want to talk about it, or would you prefer some quiet time to process?"

Partner B: "I think I need some time to wrap my head around this before I can really talk about it."

Partner A: "That makes sense. I'll give you some space. Is there anything practical I can take care of for you right now? I'm happy to handle dinner and the kids' bedtime routine tonight."

Partner B: "That would actually help a lot. Thank you for understanding."

Partner A: "Of course. And whenever you're ready to talk—whether that's later tonight or tomorrow or whenever—I'm here. There's no rush. In the meantime, would it help if I just sat with you for a bit, or would you prefer to be alone?"

This dialogue demonstrates presence without pressure, practical support, and attunement to the stressed partner's specific needs in the moment.

When Stress Becomes Overwhelming: Recognizing the Need for Additional Support

While many stressors can be effectively managed within the relationship, some situations require additional resources. Recognizing when stress has exceeded your coping capacity as a couple is an important aspect of relationship health.

Signs Additional Support May Be Needed:

- Stress is consistently interfering with basic functioning (sleep, appetite, ability to work)
- Relationship communication has broken down around stress-related issues
- Unhealthy coping mechanisms (substance use, aggression) are emerging
- One or both partners feel hopeless about the situation improving
- The supporting partner is experiencing significant compassion fatigue or secondary stress

- The same stress patterns continue despite your best efforts to change them

Types of Additional Support:

Professional Help: Couples therapy, individual counseling, or specialized support for specific stressors (financial counseling, grief support, etc.)

Community Resources: Support groups, religious/spiritual communities, or community organizations that address specific challenges

Practical Assistance: Hired help, family support, or community services that reduce practical burdens during overwhelming periods

Temporary Accommodations: Adjustments to work schedules, living arrangements, or commitments that create space for stress recovery

Exercise: Creating Your Stress Support Network Map
Time needed: 30-45 minutes **Materials**: Large paper, colored markers
This exercise helps couples identify and organize potential support resources:
Draw a circle in the center of the paper representing your relationship.
Around this circle, create sections for different types of potential support:

- Professional resources

- Family members

- Friends

- Community organizations

- Workplace supports

- Online resources

In each section, list specific resources available to you, including:
- Names and contact information

- Types of support they can provide

- Any access information (cost, location, hours)

- Discuss which resources you would activate for different types of stressors.

- Identify any gaps in your support network and discuss how you might fill them.

Keep this map accessible for reference during high-stress periods when problem solving capacity may be reduced.

Dialogue Scripts: Stress Communication in Action

Here are examples of effective stress-related communication in various scenarios:

When communicating your own stress: "I'm noticing I'm feeling really stressed right now about this deadline. I'm not looking for solutions necessarily, but I wanted to let you know that if I seem distracted or irritable, it's not about you or us—I'm just carrying this work pressure. What would help most is if I could have an hour to focus tonight, and then maybe we could take a short walk together afterward to reconnect."

When checking in about partner's stress: "I've noticed you seem tense since that phone call earlier. I'm here if you want to talk about it, or if there's something else that would be more helpful right now. No pressure either way—I just want you to know I'm tuned in and care about what you're experiencing."

When stress is affecting the relationship: "I think we might be getting caught in our stress pattern again—where I get anxious and seek reassurance, which makes you feel pressured and withdraw, which increases my anxiety. Could we pause and try a different approach? Maybe we both take ten minutes to do something calming separately, and then come back and try this conversation again?"

When requesting specific support: "With everything happening at work this week, I'm feeling overwhelmed. Would you be willing to handle the grocery shopping and cooking for the next few days? That would give me some breathing room to manage this project deadline. I'm happy to take those tasks back next week, or find another way to balance things that works for both of us."

When offering support: "It sounds like you're dealing with a lot right now. I want to support you in a way that actually helps. Would it be more helpful for me to listen while you process this, offer suggestions, or take something practical off your plate? I'm here for whatever would serve you best."

Chapter Reflection: Your Stress Management Journey

Take a moment to reflect on stress management in your relationship:

1. What are your current major sources of stress, both individually and as a couple?

2. How effectively are you navigating these together?

3. What stress patterns have you noticed in your relationship? How might awareness of these patterns help you interrupt unhelpful cycles?

4. Which stress management strategies—individual and relationship-focused—seem most relevant to your current situation?

5. What preventative practices could you implement to build greater stress resilience in your relationship?

6. How might you use the P.U.L.S.E. framework more

effectively to support each other during stressful periods?

The Bridge to the Next Chapter: Continuing Your P.U.L.S.E. Journey

Throughout this book, we've explored the five elements of the P.U.L.S.E. framework— Praise, Understanding, Listening, Self-regulation, and Empathy—and how they apply to various dimensions of relationship health. We've discovered how these elements work together to create connection, navigate conflict, build intimacy, support growth, and manage stress.

In our final chapter, we'll explore how to integrate these elements into an ongoing practice that evolves with your relationship. We'll look at how to sustain your P.U.L.S.E. journey through different relationship seasons and challenges, creating a partnership that continues to grow in depth, resilience, and joy over time.

But before we move on, I encourage you to begin implementing the stress management practices in this chapter. Remember that how you navigate stress together is one of the most powerful predictors of long-term relationship satisfaction. Each time you support each other effectively through a stressful period, you're not just solving an immediate problem—you're building confidence in your ability to face life's challenges as a team, strengthening the foundation of trust and security that allows your relationship to thrive even under pressure.

LOVE WITH P.U.L.S.E.

KEEP GOING AFTER THE CHAPTER ENDS

- Guided Video Exercises
- Printable Worksheets
- Real-Life Tools You Can Use Today

Turn what you just read into what you can actually do — right now.

Dr. Ashley R. Bryant

Creator of the P.U.L.S.E. Framework & Author of Love With P.U.L.S.E.

Already finished the book? Scan to access every chapter's bonus content in one place.

Chapter 15
The P.U.L.S.E. Journey Continues

Throughout this book, we've explored the transformative power of the P.U.L.S.E. framework—Praise, Understanding, Listening, Self-regulation, and Empathy—and how these five elements work together to create relationships that don't just survive but truly thrive. We've discovered practical applications for these principles across the full spectrum of relationship experiences, from everyday interactions to major challenges, from conflict resolution to celebration, from individual growth to shared resilience.

As we conclude our exploration, this final chapter focuses on integrating these elements into an ongoing practice that evolves with your relationship. We'll look at how to sustain your P.U.L.S.E. journey through different relationship seasons and challenges, creating a partnership that continues to grow in depth, connection, and joy over time.

The Integration Challenge: From Principles to Practice

Learning relationship principles is one thing; integrating them into the fabric of your daily life together is another. Many couples experience an initial surge of enthusiasm and improvement after learning new relationship skills, only to gradually drift back to old patterns as the demands of life take over or the novelty wears off.

The key to lasting transformation isn't perfection—it's integration and consistent practice, even when it's imperfect. Just as a musician doesn't master an instrument through occasional intense practice sessions but through regular, consistent engagement, relationship mastery comes through ongoing attention and practice.

Case Study: The Integration Journey

When Amir and Elena completed their first relationship workshop, they returned home energized and equipped with new tools. For the first few weeks, they diligently practiced their new communication skills, had regular check-ins, and noticed significant improvements in their connection.

Gradually, however, work deadlines, family obligations, and everyday stressors began to crowd out their intentional practice. They found themselves slipping back into old patterns—interrupting during discussions, becoming defensive when challenged, forgetting to acknowledge each other's efforts.

Rather than seeing this as failure, they recognized it as a natural part of the learning process. They developed a more sustainable approach: integrating smaller practices into their daily routines, setting realistic expectations for busy periods, creating visual reminders of key principles, and scheduling regular "relationship tune-ups" to refocus on their priorities.

Three years later, they described their P.U.L.S.E. practice not as something they "do" but as something they "live"—an integrated approach to their relationship that had become second nature through consistent, imperfect practice over time.

The P.U.L.S.E. Integration Framework

To help you move from understanding these principles to living them consistently, here's a practical framework for integration:

1. Start Small and Build

Rather than trying to transform everything at once, focus on integrating one element or practice at a time until it becomes more natural before adding others.

Integration Strategy: - Choose one P.U.L.S.E. element that would most benefit your relationship right now - Select a single, specific practice related to that element -

Implement this practice consistently for 2-3 weeks before adding another - Gradually build your repertoire of practices as each becomes more habitual

2. Create Environmental Supports

Your physical environment and daily routines can either support or hinder your relationship intentions. Designing your environment to prompt desired behaviors increases success.

Integration Strategy:

- Place visual reminders of P.U.L.S.E. principles in spaces you frequently see

- Set regular calendar reminders for check-ins or practices

- Create physical spaces that support connection (comfortable conversation areas, distraction free zones)

- Use technology intentionally to support your relationship goals (shared calendars, appreciation text reminders)

3. Develop Trigger-Response Plans

Identify specific challenging situations and plan alternative responses in advance, making it easier to implement new behaviors when emotions are high.

Integration Strategy:

- Identify recurring trigger situations in your relationship
- For each trigger, create a specific alternative response based on P.U.L.S.E. principles
- Practice these responses mentally or through role-play when calm
- Debrief after real situations to refine your approach

4. Establish Reflection Rhythms

Regular reflection helps you assess what's working, what isn't, and how to adjust your approach for greater effectiveness.

Integration Strategy:

- Daily: Brief end-of-day appreciation exchange
- Weekly: Short check-in on relationship quality and practice implementation
- Monthly: Deeper conversation about relationship patterns and growth areas
- Quarterly: Comprehensive review of your relationship journey and P.U.L.S.E. practice

5. Create Accountability Structures

External accountability increases follow-through on intentions, especially when forming new habits.

Integration Strategy:

- Share your relationship intentions with trusted friends who can provide supportive accountability

- Consider working with a couples therapist or relationship coach for periodic check-ins

- Join or form a couple's group focused on relationship growth

- Create mutual accountability agreements within your relationship

Exercise: Your P.U.L.S.E. Integration Plan

Time needed: 60-90 minutes Materials: Paper and pens, calendar

This exercise helps couples create a sustainable plan for integrating P.U.L.S.E. principles into daily life:

Together, review each element of the P.U.L.S.E. framework and discuss:

- Which elements feel most natural in our relationship currently?

- Which elements would most benefit from additional attention?

- What specific practices from this book resonated

most strongly with us?

Create your integration plan:
Select 1-2 practices to begin implementing immediately
Identify specific times, places, and triggers for these practices
Design environmental supports and reminders
Establish your reflection rhythm (daily, weekly, monthly)
Determine how you'll hold yourselves accountable
Anticipate challenges:
- What barriers might interfere with consistent practice?

- What strategies could help you overcome these barriers?

- How will you support each other when motivation wanes?

Schedule your first three reflection conversations in your calendar.
Create a visual reminder of your selected practices to place somewhere you'll see daily.

P.U.L.S.E. Through the Seasons of Relationship

Relationships naturally move through different seasons, each with unique challenges and opportunities. The application of P.U.L.S.E. principles evolves as your relationship journey unfolds.

New Relationships: Building the Foundation

In early relationship stages, P.U.L.S.E. practices help establish healthy patterns before problematic dynamics become entrenched.

Focus Areas:

- Praise: Developing the habit of noticing and expressing appreciation before it's eroded by familiarity

- Understanding: Creating a foundation of knowledge about each other's histories, values, and needs

- Listening: Establishing attentive listening patterns before communication shortcuts develop

- Self-regulation: Learning each other's triggers and developing regulation strategies together

- Empathy: Building the capacity to see beyond your own experience even when differences emerge
Established Relationships: Deepening and Refreshing

In long-term partnerships, P.U.L.S.E. practices help prevent stagnation and reignite connection that may have become routine.

Focus Areas:

- Praise: Finding fresh aspects to appreciate rather

than taking familiar qualities for granted

- Understanding: Continuing to update your knowledge as your partner evolves over time

- Listening: Renewing curious attention rather than assuming you already know what they'll say

- Self-regulation: Addressing entrenched triggers and reaction patterns that have developed

- Empathy: Deepening empathic connection beyond surface understanding

Relationships in Crisis: Healing and Rebuilding

During relationship challenges or after injuries, P.U.L.S.E. practices provide a pathway for repair and renewal.

Focus Areas:

- Praise: Reconnecting with what you value about each other despite current difficulties

- Understanding: Seeking to comprehend how the crisis is experienced from each perspective

- Listening: Creating safe space for painful truths to be expressed and heard

- Self-regulation: Managing intense emotions that arise during healing processes

- Empathy: Finding compassion for each other's pain, even when you've contributed to it

Transitional Periods: Navigating Change Together

During major life transitions (parenthood, career changes, empty nest, retirement),

P.U.L.S.E. practices help couples adapt while maintaining connection.

Focus Areas:

- Praise: Acknowledging each other's efforts in adapting to new circumstances

- Understanding: Updating your knowledge of each other as roles and identities shift

- Listening: Creating space to process the emotional impact of transitions

- Self-regulation: Managing the stress and uncertainty that often accompany change

- Empathy: Recognizing that transitions may affect each partner differently and at different paces

When Practice Falters: Compassionate Recovery

Even with the best intentions, there will be times when your P.U.L.S.E. practice falters.

Perhaps a major life stressor overwhelms your capacity, health issues interfere, or you simply drift away from intentional practice over time. How you respond to these inevitable lapses significantly impacts your long-term relationship journey.

The Recovery Cycle:

Recognition Without Judgment: Noticing the drift from intentional practice without harsh self-criticism or partner-blame.

Compassionate Reset: Approaching the situation with kindness toward yourselves and each other, recognizing that imperfection is part of the human relationship journey.

Curious Exploration: Investigating what contributed to the practice lapse—was it external circumstances, internal resistance, or perhaps practices that weren't sustainable?

Adjusted Restart: Beginning again with practices appropriately calibrated to your current circumstances and learnings.

Preventative Planning: Identifying what might help maintain practice through similar challenges in the future.

Dialogue Example: Compassionate Recovery

Partner A: "I've noticed we've really drifted from our connection practices these past few months. Our check-ins have become sporadic, and I feel like we're not really listening to each other the way we were before."

Partner B: "You're right. With everything that's been happening with my parent's health situation, I think we've both been in survival mode."

Partner A: "Absolutely, and I don't think either of us should feel bad about that. We've been doing our best during a really challenging time. I'm wondering if we might think about how to restart some of our practices in a way that feels manageable right now?"

Partner B: "I'd like that. Maybe we could begin with something simple, like our appreciation practice at dinner? That always helped me feel more connected without requiring a lot of extra energy."

Partner A: "That sounds perfect. And maybe we could talk about what might help us maintain at least some basic practices the next time we're in a challenging period like this?"

This dialogue demonstrates recognition without blame, compassion for the circumstances, and a collaborative approach to restarting practices in a sustainable way.

Deepening Your Practice: Advanced P.U.L.S.E. Integration

As you become more comfortable with basic P.U.L.S.E. practices, you can explore more advanced integration that takes your relationship to new levels of connection and resilience.

Advanced Integration Approaches:

Cross-Element Integration: Deliberately combining multiple P.U.L.S.E. elements in single practices, such as empathic listening exercises that also incorporate self regulation techniques.

Contextual Adaptation: Developing specialized applications of P.U.L.S.E. principles for your specific relationship challenges or circumstances.

Teaching and Mentoring: Sharing your P.U.L.S.E. journey with others, which deepens your own integration through the process of articulating and demonstrating these principles.

Value Alignment: Explicitly connecting P.U.L.S.E. practices to your core values and relationship vision, strengthening motivation for consistent practice.

Creative Expression: Developing personalized rituals, symbols, or practices that express P.U.L.S.E. principles in ways uniquely meaningful to your relationship.

Exercise: Relationship Vision Integration
Time needed: 60 minutes Materials: Your relationship vision statement (if previously created), paper and pens

This exercise helps couples connect their P.U.L.S.E. practice to their deeper relationship vision:
Together, articulate or review your relationship vision—the essence of what you want to create together and the qualities you want your partnership to embody. For each element of the P.U.L.S.E. framework, discuss:

- How does this element contribute to our larger vision?

- What specific practices related to this element would most powerfully move us toward our vision?

- How might we adapt these practices to more perfectly align with our unique relationship values and goals?

Create a visual representation that connects your vision to specific P.U.L.S.E. practices—perhaps a mind map, collage, or other creative format that resonates with you. Display this representation where you'll regularly see it, using it as both inspiration and practical reminder.

The Ripple Effect: P.U.L.S.E. Beyond Your Relationship

As you integrate P.U.L.S.E. principles more deeply into your relationship, you'll likely notice these elements influencing other areas of your life as well. The skills of praising, understanding, listening, self-regulating, and empathizing enhance all human connections—with children, family members, friends, and colleagues.

Many couples find that their P.U.L.S.E. practice creates positive ripples that extend far beyond their relationship:

Parenting: Children who observe and experience these principles in their parents' relationship learn powerful models for their own future relationships.

Family Dynamics: Extended family interactions often improve as couples bring P.U.L.S.E. skills to challenging family situations.

Friendships: The capacity for deep listening and empathy enhances the quality and depth of friendships.

Professional Relationships: Communication skills developed through P.U.L.S.E. practice frequently translate to more effective workplace interactions.

Community Impact: Couples with strong relationship skills often become resources and models for others in their communities.

Exercise: Your P.U.L.S.E. Influence
Time needed: 30 minutes Materials: Paper and pens
This reflective exercise helps couples recognize the broader impact of their relationship practice:
Draw a circle in the center of a paper representing your relationship.

Around this circle, draw additional circles representing other relationships and contexts in your lives.
For each surrounding circle, discuss:
- How have P.U.L.S.E. principles from our relationship practice influenced this area?

- What positive changes have we noticed in these relationships as our own relationship practice has deepened?

- What additional opportunities exist to bring these principles into this context?

Reflect on how your relationship growth creates value not just for yourselves but for your broader community and world.

Your Continuing Journey: A Lifelong Practice

As we conclude this book, remember that mastering the P.U.L.S.E. framework isn't a destination but a lifelong journey. The depth and application of these principles can continue to evolve throughout your relationship, offering new insights and growth opportunities at each stage.

The most fulfilling relationships aren't those that achieve perfection but those that embrace the ongoing process of learning, growing, and deepening connection. Each time you practice praise, understanding, listening, self-regulation, or empathy—even imperfectly—you strengthen the foundation of your relationship and increase your capacity for meaningful connection.

Final Reflection Questions:

As you look ahead to your continuing P.U.L.S.E. journey, consider these questions:

1. Which element of the P.U.L.S.E. framework has been most transformative for your relationship so far?

2. What specific practice from this book do you most want to integrate into your daily relationship life?

3. How might your relationship look and feel one year from now if you consistently apply these principles?

4. What support structures will help you maintain your practice through challenges and transitions?

5. How might you continue to deepen your understanding and application of these principles over time?

A Final Word of Encouragement

Thank you for joining me on this exploration of the P.U.L.S.E. framework. By investing time and attention in understanding these principles, you've already demonstrated your commitment to creating a relationship that truly thrives.

Remember that the journey toward a deeply connected, resilient, and joyful partnership

isn't about perfection—it's about presence, intention, and consistent practice. There will be moments of beautiful connection and moments of frustrating setback. Both are part of the path.

What matters most is not that you implement these principles flawlessly, but that you continue to turn toward each other with openness, compassion, and a willingness to grow. Each time you choose praise over criticism, understanding over assumption, listening over dismissal, self-regulation over reactivity, or empathy over indifference, you strengthen the bonds that make your relationship not just enduring but truly life enhancing. May your P.U.L.S.E. journey bring you deeper connection, greater resilience, and abundant joy as you continue to grow together in love.

Conclusion: Your P.U.L.S.E. Journey

As we reach the end of this book, I want to take a moment to acknowledge the journey we've been on together. Throughout these pages, we've explored the transformative power of the P.U.L.S.E. framework—a comprehensive approach to building and sustaining deep, meaningful connections in your relationships. We began by understanding the fundamental importance of connection in our lives—how it shapes our wellbeing, our sense of self, and our capacity for joy. We then delved into each component of the P.U.L.S.E. framework:

Praise: We discovered how genuine appreciation and acknowledgment create a foundation of positivity and goodwill in relationships, counteracting our natural negativity bias and building emotional resilience.

Understand: We explored the art of perspective-taking and the profound impact of trulyseeing the world through your partner's eyes, recognizing that understanding doesn't always mean agreement.

Listen: We learned the difference between hearing and listening, and how active, empathic listening creates a safe space for vulnerability and authentic expression.

Self-Regulate: We examined the critical skill of managing our own emotional responses, especially during challenging moments, allowing us to respond thoughtfully rather than react impulsively.

Empathize: We uncovered the transformative power of emotional attunement—feeling with our partners rather than just for them—and how this creates the deepest form of connection.

Beyond these core components, we explored how to apply the P.U.L.S.E. framework to various relationship contexts:

navigating conflict, building intimacy, creating shared vision, cultivating resilience, celebrating wins, supporting mental and emotional wellbeing, and managing stress together.

The Integration of Science and Practice

Throughout this book, I've woven together both the science of relationships and practical, actionable strategies. The research is clear: healthy relationships aren't just nice to have—they're essential to our physical and emotional wellbeing. Studies consistently show that the quality of our close relationships is one of the strongest predictors of happiness, health, and longevity.

The P.U.L.S.E. framework isn't just a collection of nice ideas—it's grounded in decades of research from attachment theory, interpersonal neurobiology, positive psychology, and couples therapy. When you practice these skills, you're engaging in evidence-based approaches that have been shown to strengthen bonds, improve communication, and deepen intimacy.

Your Ongoing Journey

As you close this book, remember that mastering the P.U.L.S.E. framework isn't a destination but a journey. These skills develop over time with consistent practice and intention. There will be moments of beautiful connection and moments of disconnect.

There will be days when these practices feel natural and effortless, and days when they feel challenging and elusive.

This is normal. The goal isn't perfection but progress—a gradual shift toward more conscious, connected relating. I encourage you to be patient with yourself and your partner as you implement these practices. Start small. Choose one element of the framework that resonates most strongly with you, and fo cus on integrating it into your daily interactions. Notice the impact. Then, gradually incorporate the other elements.

A Few Final Thoughts

As we conclude, I'd like to leave you with a few final reflections:

Love is both a feeling and a practice. While the feeling of love may naturally ebb and flow, the practice of love—the daily choices to turn toward each other, to remain curious, to offer kindness and understanding—can remain constant. The P.U.L.S.E. framework gives you concrete ways to practice love, especially during those times when the feeling might be temporarily obscured by life's challenges. Small moments matter. Research shows that relationships thrive not primarily through grand gestures but through the accumulation of small, positive interactions—the brief touch as you pass in the hallway, the attentive question about your partner's day, the moment of genuine appreciation for something they did. These micro-moments of connection, practiced consistently, create a relationship that feels safe, supportive, and deeply satisfying.

Your relationship is a creative act. You and your partner are co-creating your relationship every day through your choices, your words, your actions, and your presence. The P.U.L.S.E. framework offers you tools for this creation, but the unique expression of your relationship will be yours alone—a reflection of your values, your histories, your dreams, and your love for each other.

LOVE WITH P.U.L.S.E.

KEEP GOING AFTER THE CHAPTER ENDS

- Guided Video Exercises
- Printable Worksheets
- Real-Life Tools You Can Use Today

Turn what you just read into what you can actually do — right now.

Dr. Ashley R. Bryant

Creator of the P.U.L.S.E. Framework & Author of Love With P.U.L.S.E.

Already finished the book? Scan to access every chapter's bonus content in one place.

Afterword

As you move forward from these pages, I invite you to approach your relationship with renewed intention and hope. Whether you're currently navigating challenges or simply seeking to deepen an already strong connection, the practices in this book can help you create a relationship that is not just surviving but truly thriving—one characterized by deep understanding, authentic communication, emotional safety, and enduring love. The journey of love is one of the most profound adventures we undertake as human beings. It asks much of us—courage, vulnerability, patience, growth—but it offers even more in return: the joy of being truly known and accepted, the comfort of genuine companionship, the strength that comes from facing life's challenges together, and the profound privilege of witnessing another person's journey through life up close. May your P.U.L.S.E. journey bring you and your partner closer, deeper, and more fully into the experience of love—not just as a feeling but as a way of being together in this world. With warmth and gratitude for allowing me to be part of your relationship journey,

Ashley Bryant, PhD

www.ingramcontent.com/pod-product-compliance
Lightning Source LLC
Chambersburg PA
CBHW052027030426
42337CB00027B/4900